10637074

THE LANDLORDS'
&
TENANTS' HANDBOOK,

A Guide to the Letting
of Residential Property

Alan Matthews

FHB

© Fitzwarren Publishing 1995

Published by
Fitzwarren Publishing,
P.O. Box 6887,
London N19 3TG

ISBN 0 9524812 1 9

A CIP catalogue record for this book is available from the British Library

All rights reserved. No part of this publication may be reproduced in any material form (including photocopying or storing it in any medium by electronic means and whether or not transiently or incidentally to some other use of this publication) without the written permission of the copyright owner except in accordance with the Copyright, Designs and Patents Act 1988 or under the terms of a licence issued by the Copyright Licensing Agency Limited, 90 Tottenham Court Road, London, W1P 9HE, England. Applications for the copyright owner's written permission to reproduce any part of this publication should be addressed to the publisher.

Warning: The doing of an unauthorised act in relation to a copyright work may result in both a civil claim for damages and criminal prosecution.

Printed and bound by UTL Ltd, London W1

Alan Matthews is a pseudonym

CONTENTS

Contents

Preface

PREFACE

The landlord and tenant relationship is one that frequently draws the parties into conflict. In any busy county court at least one day a week will be devoted to possession actions. This is the most prolific area for contested litigation: more so than divorce, employment or consumer disputes. I suspect that part of the reason for this is the fact that it involves two people owning what each would consider primarily theirs. The landlord, who has probably invested a lot of money and effort in a property, thinks of it as his subject to another person's temporary privilege of being able to live there. On the other hand the tenant thinks of the same place as his home and the landlord's rights over it as very much secondary to his own. Complicated legislation attempts to regulate these respective claims. This combination of an inherently fraught situation and laws that many, including lawyers, do not entirely understand gives rise to so much litigation.

A lot of subsequent problems can avoided by following correct procedures at the stage of granting the tenancy. A fair proportion of landlord and tenant disputes are contested because someone has made a mess of serving a notice. Others arise because whilst there has been no "legal" error, the landlord has obviously not given any thought to the responsibility, let alone the risks, he has taken on by letting property. What I attempt to do in this book is guide both landlords and tenants through the problems and point out the responsibilities, legal and non-legal alike, of letting property. I hope that I will have said something of use to both those personally involved and those, such as letting agents, who advise them.

Certain areas which the title of this book might indicate it deals with are not covered. The most important of these is perhaps council housing. This topic is governed by a different set of laws. The practical problems facing a small private landlord are obviously vastly different from those which might affect a local authority. Similarly outside the scope of this book are long leases. In England and Wales most "owners" of flats have the benefits of such leases. The freehold owner's only entitlements are to a ground rent, sometimes service charges and a theoretical right to possession of the flat at the need of the lease. Most lessees of such flats understandably do not think of themselves as tenants at all. The relevant law and practical consideration are again very different from those which affect private short term tenancies. Agricultural tenancies are also not dealt with although they often comprise residential premises. Again separate law and different practical problems would mean, if those tenancies were included, substantial reference to areas outside the interest of what I presume the bulk of the readership of this book will be. Although there are overlaps, the law relating to all types of tenancies is different in Scotland and Northern Ireland and the test is based purely on the law of England and Wales.

One matter which may have caused minor offence to some people who read this book is the fact that I have when it is necessary to refer to a hypothetical person invariably used the masculine: "he", "his" or "him". It is an established usage but one which is sexist and with which I feel slightly uncomfortable. There are three possible ways around it, each involving an alternative to "he". Firstly, "he or she": this is long-winded and can in places add yet more complexity to already difficult concepts that I attempt to explain in the simplest possible terms. Secondly, "they": this however when used of a singular person is grammatically incorrect and can lead to sentence construction that grates on the reader. Thirdly, "she": this seemed to me equally sexist without even the excuse of established usage to justify it. Perhaps though in the next edition I will use the feminine in an attempt at least to redress the balance!

More importantly, I would provide a word of caution about the book's coverage of the law. Landlord and tenant is an area of law that has spawned a vast amount of learning. The leading textbook on it runs to four volumes and around 3,000 pages. Whilst obviously a fair proportion of that concerns areas entirely outside the compass of this book, it gives some indication of how condensed and selective a summary this is. That and the fact that laws frequently change make it most important that this book be regarded as a guide to, rather than a bible of, residential tenancies. It should be regarded as a starting point and if there is any doubt or ambiguity about what I have said a more definitive source of the law or better still a solicitor should be consulted. I have attempted to state the law as it stood on 1 January 1995.

The text is divided into sections addressed primarily to landlords and tenants. The initial section in each chapter is directed to landlords. In those initial sections I deal with many issues that are likely to be common to both parties. I suspect very few readers would feel constrained from reading what I address to the party they are not. Just in case this book has attracted the absurdly over-scrupulous, I would assure them it has not been my intention to restrict the practical use of either the landlord's or tenant's sections entirely to those to whom they are apparently addressed.

1. INTRODUTION: WHETHER TO RENT A PROPERTY

From the Landlord's Perspective

The pros and cons of letting

The number of private individuals letting property has risen substantially in recent years. The main reason for this has been the slump in house prices. Frequently people wishing to move realised that if they sold their homes they would have to accept less than they had paid when they bought the properties. Accordingly many decided to buy new properties but rent their former homes while awaiting an a turn around in the market.

This course has also been made more attractive by the provisions of the Housing Act 1988. The legislation in force before that Act meant that it was difficult for landlords to regain possession of their properties at the end of the terms for which they had been let. Further the tenant was legally entitled to apply for a "fair" rent, which would usually be a fraction of the market rent. Horror stories abounded of people who had let their homes supposedly for a few months at a substantial rent only to find that they had "sitting tenants" who could remain there for life paying a pittance.

Even under the Housing Act, which applies to tenancies granted after 14 January 1989, there are formalities with which landlords must comply strictly if they are not run the risk of losing the right to recover their properties. These are explained on pages 20 to 21. The question whether the tenancy was granted before 15 January 1989 has a tremendous effect on the respective legal rights of landlords and tenants. This book will talk about tenancies granted before or after that date. Lawyers usually refer to *protected tenancies* or *Rent Act tenancies*, being ones granted before that date and *assured tenancies* or *Housing Act tenancies* being ones granted after it.

Is a property suitable for letting?

Typically tenants will be young, single, not particularly well off people who do not see the property as being a permanent home. Often sharing arrangements will be made which involve people who do not know each other very well living in the same house. Such tenants may well spend less time at home than would a family. So some factors which could substantially affect the value of a house when it is being sold may have less bearing on the rental value. These might include:

- A quiet location;
- Structural soundness;
- Proximity of good schools; and
- Size of rooms.

However such a lifestyle may make more significant other factors such as:

- Proximity to public transport (in London, being close to a tube station is particularly important);
- Number of rooms;
- Having more than one bathroom/shower-room and a separate toilet; and
- Proximity to local amenities such as shops.

Annual rents very roughly average around 10% of properties' freehold (or in the case of flats, long leasehold) value.

Two hypothetical examples may illustrate these principles:

1. 41a, Wilson Road, Stratford, London E15

This is a four bedroom flat with a lounge, bathroom, kitchen and separate toilet, above shops on a major road, five minutes walk from Stratford British Rail and tube station. Such a flat might sell for about £70,000. Applying the 10% principle, the starting point for the rent would be around £7,000 per year. However because of the number of rooms it is likely that at least four tenants would live there. The separate toilet would make communal living a little easier than if they all had to share. They would be attracted all the more because of the flat being near the shops and particularly the particularly the tube. It would not be difficult to find four people willing to pay at least £45 per week each to live in such a flat. That translates into a rent of £180 per week or £9,360 per year.

2. Heath Cottage, Aldenham, Herts

This is a two bedroom cottage with a through lounge in a south Hertfordshire village to which there is little public transport. If it were sold, it would probably be worth around £100,000. However finding tenants willing to pay £10,000 per year for it could prove very difficult. It would be ideal for a couple with a young child. However if such people are able to afford a rent of nearly £200 per week, they would probably prefer to buy a place of their own. In this situation the landlord may well have to settle for a rent of less than 10%, say £8,500 per year, or £163 per week.

Another factor which affects whether or not renting is likely to be profitable is the level of mortgage interest rates. At the time of writing these are around 7%. Most privately-owned properties will be mortgaged to banks or building societies. The amount of interest payable on that mortgage will have to be balanced against the rent received. If the mortgage is less than 100% of the value of the home, the landlord will have to take into account the notional amount of income he would be receiving were he to invest the surplus he would get on sale after repaying the mortgage. On the other hand, mortgages nowadays frequently amount to more than 100% of the value of the property. This syndrome, often known as *"negative equity"*, arises where the value of a property falls after it has been mortgaged, making the amount of money secured on it more than the property is worth. In this situation the prospective landlord also has to consider the amount of interest he would have to pay on money he borrowed to enable him to repay the mortgage. As he would no longer have the property on which to secure that loan, he would almost certainly pay a rate higher than was charged under the mortgage.

This can be illustrated by looking at the positions of the owners of the above examples.

1. Mrs Healey

Mrs Healey owns 41a Wilson Road. She bought the flat at the height of the "boom" for £83,000 with 100% mortgage. The interest on her mortgage is at the moment £6,000: substantially less than the rent she would receive. However if she sold the flat for £70,000, she would still have to pay interest on the £13,000 shortfall. On an unsecured loan of that amount she might have to pay 15%, an annual sum of around £2,000. Thus she would only be reducing her interest payments by (£6,000- £2,000) £4,000 if she sold the flat, which is more than £5,000 less than she would receive by way of rent.

2. Mr Barber

Mr Barber owns Heath Cottage. Despite its greater value- £100,000, he only has a £92,000 mortgage on it, on which he pays interest of £6,500 per year. If he sells it, he would have £8,000 to invest. He is a cautious man and would merely put in the building society where it might pay him 5%, that's £400 per year. He would therefore be saving £8,400 per year, only £100 less than he might be receiving in rent.

In this situation Mrs Healey would be well advised to let her property out. Mr Barber would not. As she does therefore decide to let it she and her property will form the basis for a number of other examples throughout this book. Conversely Mr Barber decides to sell and, for the sake of keeping a small cast, this book will have him do so to Mrs Healey. She will go and live there and in due course decide to let the spare bedroom.

Landlords inevitably have to pay other expenses. Insurance of the property (though not the contents), water rates and most repairs are the landlord's responsibility in a normal residential tenancy. Depending on the area and the condition of the premises these might take up 15% of the rent. Some landlords may elect to use agents to find tenants in the first place and to subsequently manage the property. Fees particularly for managing the property, can be substantial. The advantages and disadvantages of using agents are discussed on pages 44 to 46.

To keep the examples given above as simple as possible no account has been taken of the cost of furnishing the properties, which is discussed at pages 37 to 38. The provision of furniture is rarely more than a marginal cost to the landlord compared with those connected with the property itself. When considering mortgage repayments the above examples were also restricted to interest. There will in practice either be a capital repayment to be made along with the interest or a premium on the endowment policy. In the long term these payments can be disregarded as the landlord is "buying" something with them, either a capital interest in the property itself or the benefit of the endowment. However for a person with cash flow difficulties, being released from the need to make those payments may be a welcome relief.

It should also be borne in mind that a rental income can never be completely secure. There is always the possibility that the tenants will fail to pay the rent, damage the property or cause the landlord to run up substantial legal fees to get them out. If these things happen, the bank lending money on the property will show scant sympathy to a landlord who as a result defaults on his mortgage repayments.

If despite all this, the landlord does make a profit on renting the property, he will have to pay tax on it. Whilst mentioning tax, prospective landlords should bear in mind that their mortgage repayments will be greater once they no longer live in a property. *Mortgage Interest Relief at Source (MIRAS)* is applied to mortgages which enable people to buy their homes. This results in a saving equivalent to the lowest rate of income tax (currently 20%) being given on interest payments on the first £30,000 of the mortgage. With an interest rate of 7% this is £420 per year. The mortgage repayments will increase by that amount. However if the landlord does make a profit from renting, the entire mortgage interest payment will be taken into account in calculating his tax liability.

With all these factors in mind Mr Barber would seem to have very little to gain by renting out Grove Cottage. Inevitably his expenses would be greater than the rental income. Probably the capital value of the property will increase over the next few years, though the chances are it will not do so to such an extent as to cancel out his losses. On the other hand Mrs Healey will almost certainly be better off renting rather than selling 41a Wilson Road: even after paying all possible expenses, including agents if she chooses to use them, she will make a few thousand pounds profit.

From the Tenant's Perspective

Financial considerations

For many tenants the decision whether to rent or buy is made for them: by the banks and building societies who will not advance them enough money to buy. As has already been said, the typical tenant is young and single and does not see his rented property as a long term home. This should be qualified by saying that this book is only concerned with privately let homes. Council housing, although outside the ambit of this book, of course provides secure homes for many millions of families.

Whilst the factors which might affect whether someone sells or lets property are primarily financial, the decision from the point of the view of the prospective tenant will be far more influenced by personal matters.

The fall in housing prices has, thankfully, made home-ownership accessible to a wider range of people than was the case in the mid 1980's. There are many perfectly reasonable flats available particularly away from the south-east of England for under £20,000. In London about £30,000 seems to be the starting price for an inhabitable property. With mortgages of three times an individual's or two and a half times a couple's joint salary readily available, buying a home is a viable option for the vast majority of the working population.

Applying the principles discussed in relation to landlords, with mortgage interest rates around 7% and a typical rent 10% of a property's value, buying is likely to be more attractive if financial factors alone are taken into account. Even bearing in mind the other costs of owning, such as insurance, repairs, water rates and capital repayments owning a home will generally not cost more than renting the same one over an extended period.

However it should be borne in mind that mortgage rates fluctuate. It was not long ago that they were virtually double what they are at the time of writing. They could go up or down in the next few years. There is little agreement amongst economists as to which is more likely. What however is self-evident is that there is more scope for them to go substantially up rather than down. They could again double from their present level. To decrease by a similar amount would mean they went down to nil: that sadly is not going to happen! Although rents to some extent follow mortgage interest rates the degree of fluctuation is much less.

It may also be possible for someone who has bought a property to offset some of the cost by letting a room in it to a lodger, a course which is discussed on pages 67 to 70.

Personal considerations

Whatever the possible financial advantages, it has to be remembered that home-ownership involves a tremendous commitment. Many young people enjoy the freedom of being able to move around with relatively little constriction. They may find a job in a different part of the country or want to move to live with a partner, they may just get fed up with their home and want somewhere different. With rented property there is unlikely to be a tie preventing them from doing that after more than a few months. Selling a property often takes far longer.

Newspapers frequently run stories of the misery of couples who have split up and yet are forced to carry on living in the same home, sometimes sharing the only bedroom, because they cannot sell it. Platonic friends can also fall out. Whilst the tensions may not be quite as horrendous as it was for a couple, they still can make life fairly unbearable. Only people who are very sure of their relationship are well advised to buy with someone to whom they are not married. Arrangements involving brothers and sisters purchasing properties together often work reasonably well. Whilst they will have as many rows as any other sharers, the underlying relationship is likely to be strong enough to prevent them seriously falling out. And the prospects of parental help is substantially enhanced when a property is going to remain entirely within the family.

Lots of people don't like the idea of living on their own. Having flat-mates should be on the whole be pleasant, someone to share the chores with, someone to talk to in the evenings. Many shared house-holds manage to become almost surrogate families. Renting a property enables people to live in, rather than being trapped in, such an environment, which is inevitably a risk if a group of people buy together.

Buying and selling can also be an expensive business. Solicitors' fees are likely to be at least £200 for both the buyer and seller. A survey might also cost the buyer that much. When a property is sold estate agents tend to charge around 2%. If the price is over £60,000, 1% stamp duty has to be paid by the buyer. If a person has owned a property for less than two or so years before selling it these costs are likely to amount to more than the saving over having rented a similar property during the same period.

2. GRANTING THE TENANCY

From the Landlord's Perspective

Preliminary considerations

Before granting the tenancy the landlord should consider the legal implications of what he is doing. This is the time when he should take professional advice or at very least triple check that he has done everything correctly. It is much easier and cheaper to avoid mistakes at this time than to put them right afterwards. In many ways granting a tenancy is just as big a step as selling a house. Almost everybody selling a house appreciates the significance of the transaction and has at least a vague idea of the dangers involved. In many ways renting is an even riskier business. Far more landlords lose out because of badly prepared tenancy agreements than sellers (or purchasers) of property do because of conveyancing problems.

Most landlords will want to ensure that they can regain possession of the property at the end of the agreed term of the tenancy. Since the 1988 Housing Act was passed this has been relatively easy so long as the landlord gets the paperwork right before granting the tenancy. Matters of detail are absolutely essential. It is possible for a landlord to find that he has given the tenant the right to remain in the property for the rest of his life simply because a notice is in the wrong form or because it is handed over too late.

Almost all residential tenancies granted by private landlords are subject to the Housing Act 1988. However if the tenancy also comprises business premises, agricultural land or a pub it will not be regarded as residential, though other statutory protection is likely to apply. Tenancies at a rent that is very high- over £25,000 per year- or very low- under £1,000 in Greater London, £250 anywhere else- are also exceptions. Generally speaking if the landlord lives in the same property there won't be a tenancy at all, merely a licence (see pages 22 to 23). However even if technically there is a tenancy, the tenant won't in that situation acquire the same rights as a tenant normally would.

There is no legal requirement for a tenancy to be granted by a written document. It can be done orally. That however is a course which from the

19

landlord's point of view has little to recommend it. Written agreements and notices are generally prepared by landlords with a view to protecting their interests. If these are dispensed with, the landlord will have lost his opportunity to do this, as well as failing to ensure there is an easily provable record of precisely what was agreed between him and the tenant.

Assured shorthold tenancies

The granting of *assured shorthold tenancies* is the most widely used way by which landlords ensure that they can get the property back. (As has already been stated, virtually all tenancies granted after 14 January 1989 are *assured tenancies*.) Any residential tenancy for six months or longer can be an assured shorthold so long as the landlord serves the correct notice. However the landlord must serve notice on the tenant that it is to be an assured shorthold before the tenancy is entered into. This means before any binding tenancy agreement is made. The landlord must not wait until the tenant actually starts living in the property. A copy of the notice that should be served appears on page 101. However the statutory instrument that decrees the information that has to be in this notice is varied from time to time and a landlord would be well advised to use an up to date form that can be bought from a law stationer. The landlord must then carefully fill in on that form the address of the property, the starting date and length of the tenancy, the date the notice was served, the parties' names and the landlord's address. If there is more than one tenant, the notice must be addressed to both or all of them. The landlord should keep a copy of the notice and make the tenant write on that copy a statement on it that he has received the original. Once that has been done the landlord and tenant should then both sign the main tenancy agreement- if there is more than one they must all sign.

The landlord's home

Where the landlord has previously lived in the property as his only or principal home or he intends to do so in the future, he can grant a *Ground 1 tenancy* (after Ground 1 of Schedule 2 to the Housing Act 1988). This form of tenancy is not used by landlords, even ones entitled to grant them, with anything like so much frequency as are assured shorthold tenancies. The main advantages to a Ground 1 tenancy are that there is no requirement for a minimum term of six months and the landlord has more flexibility in subsequently increasing the rent. Where the landlord has not previously lived in the property, granting the tenancy on the basis that the landlord intends to live there in future is obviously a potentially dangerous course. If he changes his mind and decides not to, he will have no way of forcing the tenant out.

A landlord granting a Ground 1 tenancy must serve a notice on the tenant before the beginning of the tenancy that possession may be recovered pursuant to that Ground. Again if there is more than one tenant, it must be served on all of them. This notice does not have to follow any particular wording.

> **Returning to the example of Mrs Healey and 41a Wilson R: she has lived in the property and might well decide to grant a tenancy of this sort rather than an assured shorthold tenancy. The first thing she should do is prepare this notice in blank, including space for the tenant to acknowledge receipt. She does this and it reads as follows:**
>
> **To.............**
> **This is to give you notice that I have previously occupied 41a Wilson Road, Stratford, London E15 as my only or principal home. Therefore the tenancy you intend taking of this property will be subject to Ground 1 of Schedule 2 to the Housing Act 1988 and I will be able to recover possession pursuant to that notice.**
> **Signed: A H Healey (Mrs)   landlord**
> **Date:**
> **I have received a copy of this notice on   19   before being granted any tenancy of 41a Wilson Road**
> **Signed: tenant**
>
> **She would then prepare the tenancy agreement, perhaps relying on the one contained at pages 103 to 105.**

Other ways of avoiding giving security of tenure

There are several other methods prescribed in Schedule 2 to the Housing Act 1988 that a landlord may use to avoid granting a tenancy of the sort that gives security of tenure. The only one that is likely to affect private landlords is Ground 3. This applies if the tenancy is for a specified period of up to eight months and in the previous twelve months the property had been occupied under a right to occupy it for a holiday. Under this Ground a notice similar to a Ground 1 notice has to be served. It should be noted that if the letting is granted for the purpose of enabling the tenant to occupy the property for a holiday no security of tenure will be given. Educational establishments and religious bodies and ministers are also able in some circumstances to grant tenancies which will not attract security.

Licences

People are sometimes granted a *licence* to live in a property rather than a tenancy of the property. Where that happens a completely different nomenclature is used: landlord becomes "licensor"; tenant "licensee"; rent, "licence fee". Somebody living in another person's home as a lodger is clearly a licensee rather than a tenant. However where the right to live in an entire property is granted to a person or a group of people such a right is generally regarded as a tenancy rather than a licence, even if the landlord made the tenant sign an agreement saying it was a licence.

Before the passing of the Housing Act 1988 landlords had fewer means of avoiding the legislation (the Rent Act 1977) that gave tenants considerable rights. Accordingly the use of licence agreements was common. Until 1985 the courts were surprisingly willing to uphold such agreements even in cases where objectively there would have appeared to be a tenancy. However in that year the judicial House of Lords set a precedent in considering an agreement entered into between a Mr Street and a Mrs Mountford. Under this agreement Mrs Mountford was granted a "licence" to live in a furnished room in Bournemouth. However the Lords, notwithstanding that description, decided it was in fact a tenancy. Mrs Mountford had been granted exclusive possession of that room: the landlord could not require her to share it with anybody else. That factor was all important and prevented the landlord from being able to avoid the Rent Act.

There are still a few situations where a licence will have been granted. The most obvious and important example is of course that of a lodger. Where one person lets another live in property for the purpose of him being able to do his job that too will be a licence, known as a *service licence* or *service occupancy*, not a tenancy. An example of this would be a caretaker living in the block of flats he looks after. The grey area is where a landlord lets a house to a number of different people at different times for different periods. If the people living there are left to decide amongst themselves who is to sleep in which room, there is arguably no identifiable piece of property that each could be said to have been granted a tenancy of.

Since the Housing Act 1988 was passed there has been little point in landlords claiming that what they have granted is not a tenancy. Any attempt to do so will be fraught with danger. If a dispute arises and the landlord fails to persuade the court that the agreement actually is a licence, he will have lost his opportunity to grant an assured shorthold tenancy rather than one which permits the tenants to stay indefinitely.

Company lets

Where a property is let to a limited company rather than an individual the rights given to tenants under the Housing Act 1988 will not apply. Before the Housing Act 1988 *company lets* were often used as a means to avoid the Rent Act. The prospetive tenant would be required to form or purchase a company and the landlord would then grant the tenancy to that company, which as tenant would allow its owner to live in the property. This, like the licence, is a device fraught with difficulties that landlords would now be well advised to avoid. If it subsequently appeared that the real intention was to grant a tenancy to the individual, a court might consider that there actually was a tenancy in favour of that individual.

There are however also genuine company lets under which an established company takes a tenancy of a property which it in turn lets to an employee or director. Such a letting will be outside the Housing Act 1988. The only disadvantage to the landlord in letting to a company is that if the company goes into liquidation ,it will not be possible to recover any arrears of rent.

The length of the tenancy

After deciding on the type of tenancy, the landlord will next have to choose the length of the tenancy he wishes to grant. Of course he may not find tenants willing to accept a tenancy for that term and may have to accept something other than the term he would regard as ideal. Generally speaking it is unwise to put pressure on tenants to enter into agreements for longer than they want. However reprehensible it may be, tenants will often simply leave with no forwarding address and owing rent if they are under an obligation to stay once they want to go.

The landlord will want to ensure that he does not grant such a long tenancy that he will be prevented from selling or living in the property when he wishes to. On the other hand he will not want to grant such a short tenancy that the tenants may be gone in a few weeks and he has to go to all the fuss of finding replacements.

Except for assured shorthold tenancies, which have to be for a minimum of six months, a tenancy can be for as short a term as the landlord wants. Many tenancies are in fact not for a set term at all. Instead they are granted from week to week or month to month- occasionally from quarter to quarter or year to year- and can be ended by the giving of notice on either side. (It should though be remembered that giving notice will not entitle the landlord to possession unless he can show that there is a statutory basis for possession as well.) If the landlord wishes to grant an assured shorthold tenancy to tenants who are only prepared to commit themselves to, say, three months he can get around this difficulty by granting it for six months but giving the tenants an option to quit after three months.

A landlord who is unsure of the length of time he wants to let a property for can try to persuade the tenant to accept an agreement for a specific length of time which contains a *break clause*. This clause means the landlord can on serving the appropriate notice to quit bring the tenancy to an end within the term. This is similar in effect to the option to quit after three months that could be given to assured shorthold tenants, except here of course it is the landlord who might operate it. It must be remembered though that if the landlord is able to operate the clause within six months of the tenancy commencing, it cannot be an assured shorthold tenancy, whether or not the landlord actually operates the clause.

The rent

Factors that are likely to affect the rent are discussed on pages 12 to 15. There it is suggested that a starting point for calculating rent might be 10% of the freehold value of the property. If this approach is to be used, it is first necessary to find out roughly what the freehold value is. Most estate agents will provide a free oral valuation. In quiet times some will not even be put off doing so if told the truth: that the owner is not at the moment considering selling. They will provide information in the hope that when the property is eventually sold the help they have previously provided is remembered. Indeed some will even be prepared to give an informed view of the likely market rent. Of course, a landlord using an agency to let the property will have the benefit of that agency's experience of local conditions in assessing the rent.

The 10% figure even in conjunction with the other factors discussed on pages 12 to 15 provides only a very rough indication. Looking in a local newspaper at the rents being sought for comparable properties will provide a more reliable guide. Obviously a prospective landlord who knows other people who rent property in the area will be able to ask for information from them about rent levels.

Joint landlords

If a property is jointly owned by more than one person, the principles relating to letting are much as the same as a property in single ownership. Ideally all documents should be signed by both owners. However if that causes difficulties one landlord can sign on behalf of both. This applies to initial notices, the tenancy agreement and any notices that may have to be served later under the tenancy itself.

Joint tenants

Most properties are let to more than one tenant. Tenancy agreements normally have the effect of making joint tenants *jointly and severally* liable to observe the obligations of the lease and pay the rent. The most important implication of this is that if one moves out, the other has to carry on paying the entire rent. If the landlord enters into separate agreements with each tenant, then each can only be liable in respect of his share of the obligations. Whilst doing this may prevent there being an assured tenancy altogether, it can cause confusion and uncertainty. Once tenants have become established in a property it is not a good idea for the landlord to decide who moves in with them if one leaves. Granting the lease to all the tenants jointly protects the landlord's position as far as the payment of rent is concerned and gives the tenants more autonomy in deciding matters like who should live in the property. The form of lease that appears on pages 103 to 105 provides for this course. When there is more than one tenant, all notices must be addressed to and, where appropriate, acknowledged by both or all of the tenants.

Was the tenancy granted after 14 January 1989?

In the vast majority of cases it will be perfectly obvious when the tenancy was granted. However there are a few situations in which the law will deem the tenancy to have been granted before 15 January 1989 and hence subject to the rules of the Rent Act 1977 which are generally less favourable to landlords than the Housing Act 1988. If the tenancy agreement was made before that date, then the tenancy will be subject to the Rent Act regardless of when it actually started.

A landlord who lets property to a person who previously was his tenant under a Rent Act tenancy will create another tenancy that is still subject to the Rent Act 1977 even if it were granted after 14 January 1989. This applies regardless of whether the tenancy is of a new property, whether the landlord grants the tenancy jointly with another landlord or jointly to another tenant. The only exception to this provision is if the earlier tenancy was or had been a protected shorthold tenancy.

Deposits

It is the normal practice for a landlord to seek a deposit of between a fortnight's and two months' rent from his tenants. This is done so that the landlord has a simple means of compensating himself if the tenants leave without paying their rent or if they cause damage at the property.

An inventory of the landlord's property including fixtures and fittings, and furniture if appropriate, is usually drawn up. . If anything is already broken or worn at the time the tenancy is granted, this should be noted on the inventory. The tenants should be given an opportunity to make a thorough inspection of the premises before signing the inventory. When agents deal with letting, they generally use a specialist inventory clerk. It may be worthwhile a landlord employing such a person: the resulting inventory would be much more authoritative in case of a subsequent dispute than one drawn up by the landlord himself.

It is advisable to insist on the deposit being paid and, if the payment is by cheque that clearing before the tenants move in. Once the tenancy commences it is going to be more difficult to persuade the tenants to hand over the money.

The landlord should remember though that the deposit is intended as a security and not as an interest free loan by the tenant to him. The landlord is under a moral and legal duty to pay any interest the deposit has earned to the tenant. This will usually not be a very large sum. Over the course of a year a deposit of £500 will probably only attract about £25 interest. Agreeing to pay this over will however show the tenants that the landlord intends to play fair: something that will often generate goodwill worth a lot more than £25.

References

A landlord may well feel that making some checks on a tenant's reliability is advisable. The most frequent sources of such information are employers or colleges, banks and previous landlords. Obtaining references from any of these sources can be difficult. Previous landlords will more often than not fail to reply. Banks' responses have to be expressed in very non-committal terms to avoid the possibility of breaching confidence or of saying something about which either the landlord or tenant might have a sustainable complaint. An employer's reference is likely to do no more than establish that the tenant works for who he claims to be employed by. A stamped addressed envelope is a courtesy that will increase the chances of obtaining a reply from the previous landlord and the employer. Banks would not normally expect one. Banks however will not disclose any information without their customer's permission. It will be necessary to have the tenant sign a consent to the bank doing this, which should be sent along with the request for the reference. There would be no harm in also sending at least a copy of this to the previous landlord and employer.

A reference from a previous landlord stating that the tenant has regularly been late paying his rent, and raising other complaints should be enough to put most landlords off the idea of taking that person as a tenant. However it could be unfair to deprive a person of the opportunity of a place to live because he is overdrawn at the bank or has only recently started a new job.

It may sometimes be possible to obtain references over the telephone. Banks however will not provide information without a written consent. Many will refuse to accept even a fax for this purpose, insisting on an "original" signature.

Just as effective as references in many cases is the production of documents by the tenant. If he can produce pay slips, bank statements and a rent book showing satisfactory finances over the last few months that is at least as effective as seeking that information from the people he has been dealing with. It will certainly be a lot quicker.

Replies to requests for references inevitably take a while. If the landlord is not prepared to commit himself to granting a tenancy during that period, the tenant can hardly be blamed for looking elsewhere. There is little point in granting a tenancy, then checking references. The grant of the tenancy will be irrevocable, and unsatisfactory references are not one of the basis on which possession can be obtained.

Returning to 41a Wilson Road: Mrs Healey has however decided that she will insist on written references. To save time once she starts meeting prospective tenants, she prepares letters in advance just leaving the details particular to the tenant and the date to be filled in before sending them.

1. To the bank

Dear Sir,

Re: [*Name of tenant*] and a/c no...

I understand [*name of tenant*] keeps the above account at your branch. He/she wishes to rent a flat from me at a rent of £180 per week, which he/she will share with three other tenants. I wonder if you could tell me whether he/she is good for such an amount. A prompt reply would be appreciated.

Yours faithfully,

2. To the previous landlord

Dear Sir,

Re: [*Name of tenant*] and the tenancy of [*tenant's present address*]

I understand [*name of tenant*] has been a tenant of the above property of which you are the landlord since [*date*]. I wonder if you could confirm that that is the case and that he/she has been a

satisfactory tenant. I enclose a stamped addressed envelope. A prompt reply would be appreciated.
Yours faithfully,

3. To the employer
Dear Sir,
Re: *[name of tenant]*
I understand that *[name of tenant]* has worked for you as a *[tenant's job]* for you since *[date]* and that he/she is paid a gross sum of *[tenant's wages or salary]* per week/month. He/she wishes to rent a flat from me and I would be grateful if you would confirm this information is correct. I enclose a stamped addressed envelope. A prompt reply would be appreciated.
Yours faithfully,

4. Consent form
To whom it may concern:
I hereby give consent to the disclosure to Mrs A H Healey of any financial or other information requested by way of reference as to whether or not she would be advised to grant me a tenancy of a residential property.

Sureties

Once a tenant has left a property it is all but impossible to get any rent out of him. If he leaves the property substantially in arrears, he probably will not tell the landlord of his new address. Where the landlord has taken a deposit there will be something to offset against the arrears, but it often will not be sufficient, particularly if the tenant has caused damage as well as running up arrears. Even if a recalcitrant former tenant can be traced, he may well not have the money to pay the outstanding sums. Suing him is likely to result in "good money" being thrown after "bad".

A landlord can greatly reduce the risk of this happening by insisting that the tenant provide a *surety* for the rent. This means that someone else promises the landlord that the tenant will pay the rent and any other sums owing as a result of the tenancy agreement and agrees to pay those sums if the tenant defaults on them. Typically the surety will be the tenant's parents, though sometimes employers and friends are willing to take on the job. As well as providing the landlord with a remedy if anything goes wrong, the knowledge that their parents will become involved if they misbehave, is enough to make many tenants act responsibly.

For a surety agreement to be valid, it has to be in writing and signed by the surety. It is also essential that the agreement is made before there is a binding tenancy. If it is not, the surety has not received any benefit and will not be bound by his promise to pay if the tenant defaults. It is a good idea to suggest the surety seek legal advice as there is a possibility if the surety signed the agreement without being given an opportunity to understand it, it would not be enforceable.

The surety agreement Mrs Healey prepared for her tenant's surety, whom she imagined would be one of his parents ran:
In consideration for the grant of a tenancy of 41a Wilson Road, Stratford, London E15 by Mrs A H Healey to [tenant's name] I hereby agree to indemnify Mrs A H Healey against any default in payment of rent, mesne profits, damages for use and occupation, damages for disrepair, other damages or costs she may incur as a result of the said tenancy or any further occupation of the property after the expiry of the tenancy whether under a statutory continuation thereof or not.
Signed.................................
Witnessed.............................

Mrs Healey prepared a covering letter for sending to the sureties:
Dear Mr/Mrs [name],
I understand from your son/daughter [tenant's name] that you are willing to stand surety if I grant him/her a tenancy of 41a Wilson Road, Stratford, London E15. I enclose a blank surety form for your and a witness' signature. Could I point out that this does potentially entail a substantial liability if [tenant's name] should default and you might think it appropriate to seek the advice of a solicitor before signing it.
Yours sincerely,

Even the existence of a surety cannot provide an absolute guarantee against the tenant's default. It may turn out that his parents, despite their posh sounding address, are broke. It would be possible to ask the sureties to provide references in the same way that the tenants might. However many would refuse to do this, feeling that they have done their bit by agreeing to be sureties at all.

An important notice

A landlord has to serve a notice on the tenant stating an address at which notices relating to the tenancy can be served on him. This address must be in England or Wales. Landlords living abroad will have to provide the address of an agent, who can be a friend or professional adviser, for this purpose. If this notice is not served, the landlord is not entitled to any rent until he does serve it. At the time of writing it had been held by the Court of Appeal that stating the address in the lease was sufficient to comply with this obligation. However the position is still far from clear, and landlords would be well advised to serve a notice separately when granting a new tenancy. Similarly, if a notice has not already been served during the currency of an existing tenancy, sending one to a tenant could protect the landlord's position if he has the slightest reason to think the tenant might ever default.

> **The notice Mrs Healey prepared to give her tenants read as follows:**
> **To:**
> **The tenant [or tenants], [*tenant's name or names*]:**
> **This notice is to inform you that all notices (including notices in proceedings) may be served on me at the following address:**
> **Heath Cottage,**
> **Aldenham,**
> **Hertfordshire**
> **This notice is intended to and does comply with the requirements of s48 of the Landlord and Tenant Act 1987.**
> **Signed A H Healey (Mrs) The landlord**

Other charges

A landlord inevitably incurs other costs in granting a tenancy. He may have had to advertise for tenants; he may have paid a solicitor to check the tenancy agreement for him; he may have employed an inventory clerk. Landlords do sometimes try to pass on some or all of these costs to the tenants at the start of the lease. Doing this was actually a criminal offence under the Rent Act 1977. Since the Housing Act 1988 came into force the landlord is entitled to charge the tenants a premium, which is what reimbursement for expenses amounts to. However it remains a somewhat unsavoury practice. Tenants resent it and understandably so. In some circumstances the payment of a premium may entitle the tenant to transfer the tenancy to another person without the landlord's permission. If the landlord is determined to recover his expenses he should adjust the rent appropriately. If he can't find anyone willing to pay the enhanced rent he probably wouldn't have found anyone willing to pay the premium.

Repairs

To a large extent the rules on repairing obligations are ordained by statute (s11 of the Landlord and Tenant Act 1985). Only leases of seven years or longer are excluded from these provisions. In essence the landlord is responsible for all structural repairs and for maintaining the plumbing, heating and electricity, gas and water supplies. Any attempt by the landlord to place the obligations in respect of these onto the tenant will be void.

There is no reason why the landlord cannot require the tenants to be responsible for maintaining the decoration at the premises, although this may be hard to enforce. In a lease for more than around three years it would be reasonable to require the tenants to decorate the property in the last three months of the term. In theory if the lease is silent on the point, tenants are under a duty to carry out repairs which are not specified by the Landlord and Tenant Act to be the landlord's responsibility. Repairing obligations are discussed in more detail on pages 39 to 40.

Other terms of the lease

A number of provisions that protect a landlord's interests are virtually standard in leases. The suggested form of tenancy that appears on pages 103 to 105 incorporates most of these terms. Few are likely to be objected to by tenants. However there are other matters that the landlord should consider before the tenancy agreement is completed. The landlord has to remember that once the tenants have moved in it is their home and the landlord can no longer make up rules. It is therefore vital that he impose them at this stage and incorporate them into the agreement.

Does he wish to restrict the number of people who can live or sleep in the property? Once the lease is granted there is nothing to stop the original tenant having other people move in with him. A landlord may have let a property to an individual or a couple only to find there are four or five people living on the premises. This may well result in the property suffering a great deal more wear and tear than would have been caused by the original tenant. A large and fluctuating body of overnight guests is likely to have a similarly undesirable effect. A clause in the lease imposing some sort of restriction might be advisable, and a suggested form of such a clause and others discussed in this section are also contained in the tenancy agreement on pages 103 to 105.

Does the landlord object to pets? It would usually be wise to include a prohibition on the keeping of pets without the landlord's prior permission.

If there is a garden are the tenants to be responsible for maintaining this? It would not be realistic to expect tenants to keep beautifully manicured lawns and ensure that flowerbeds are planted every year. On the other hand most tenants would be willing to accept a term that they should not allow a garden to become overgrown. If there is a garden some clause to this effect should be included in the lease.

The forfeiture clause

A *forfeiture clause* is obtained in virtually all professionally drafted leases.

Typically it would read like this:

If any part of the rent is in arrears for more than 21 days whether formally demanded or not or there is any breach of the tenant's obligations under the lease the landlord may re-enter the premises and thereupon the tenancy created by this lease will determine, but without prejudice to any other rights and remedies of the landlord.

What this legalese means is that if the tenant doesn't behave himself, he will forfeit his rights under the lease. A slightly different clause appears in the part of the draft tenancy agreement that is on page 104. On the face of it such a clause entitles the landlord to take possession of the premises as soon as the rent is three weeks in arrears or the tenant commits some other breach. In fact, where the lease is of residential premises, the landlord can't do this without a court order. The clause is though still necessary in a residential lease. If a lease of, say, a year is granted and the tenant fails to pay rent, the landlord would not be entitled to possession until the end of the year. All he could do in the meanwhile is attempt to sue the tenant for the arrears, which is not a simple or satisfactory course. The forfeiture clause has the effect that the landlord has a contractual right to possession. Once he has that right a court has a power to order possession in his favour if one of the statutory grounds for possession apply. Without that clause it will be impossible for the landlord to recover possession during the term of the lease: with the clause it will still be far from easy.

The existence of a forfeiture clause does not prevent a lease being an assured shorthold tenancy despite having the effect that a landlord can terminate the lease in less than six months.

From the Tenant's Perspective

Exempt landlords

Whilst most tenancies are assured tenancies and hence give the tenants more rights than may be specified in the tenancy agreement certain landlords are exempt from these provisions altogether. The most significant are local authorities and other government bodies. Council housing is subject to a complete different set of legislation, generally more favourable to tenants, but outside the scope of this book. Where a college grants a tenancy to a student attending a course there, that will usually be outside the legislation. Also excluded are holiday lets and lettings which include business or agricultural property.

Agreeing the terms

It should be remembered that the terms of a lease like any other bargain are a matter for negotiation rather than the *diktat* of one party. If a prospective tenant believes that the landlord is asking too high a rent then he should say so. If the landlord refuses to budge on the rent then the tenant has to decide whether to accept the higher rent or look for somewhere else. The landlord's attitude will almost certainly be determined by whether or not he is confident of finding another tenant willing to pay that rent. A tenant may be wary that if he tries to negotiate with the landlord at all, the landlord will simply refuse to grant him the tenancy. That fear may in some circumstances be legitimate. It is unlikely though that anyone who had that attitude would be a particularly pleasant person to have a landlord. Only a tenant absolutely desperate to rent a particular property should allow that sort of fear to dissuade him from politely attempting to negotiate with the landlord.

References

What is said at pages 27 to 29 about references should be particularly taken on board by tenants. A person who turns up to meet a landlord with documents that prove he is a desirable character is likely to have a considerable advantage over anyone else after the same property. If a tenant intends giving out anybody's name to be a referee, it is sensible and courteous to ask that person's permission in advance.

The effect of the tenancy agreement

Something that should not need to be emphasised is that a tenant must appreciate that once he signs an agreement he is stuck with its terms. If he has agreed to live in a property for a year, then he must assume that he is bound to pay the rent for that year even if he decides that he wants to move. Similarly if he has a beloved cat but signs a lease with a no pets clause, then he isn't going to be allowed to have moggy live with him.

For these reasons tenants should read anything they are asked to sign thoroughly. If there is something in it that they don't understand, they should get it explained to them, ideally by a solicitor; failing that by a Citizens'

Advice Bureau. It is fair to say that leases that are on standard forms produced by law stationers are unlikely to contain any unpleasant surprises unless the landlord has added to what is on the form. Forms produced by landlords or their agents may not be so even-handed.

In some circumstances a tenant may be granted security of tenure greater than appears to be the case from the lease. If the landlord does not give him a notice saying the tenancy is an assured shorthold or that the landlord may recover possession for other reasons, it may well be that the tenant is entitled to stay on at the end of the term. If the tenancy is an assured shorthold, it may be possible for the tenant to challenge the level of rent in due course. However it would not be a good idea to make assumptions based on these possibilities when deciding whether or not to enter into the tenancy agreement.

3. WHAT SHOULD BE PROVIDED UNDER THE TENANCY

From the Landlord's Perspective

Furniture

From the point of view of the legal nature of the tenancy it now makes very little difference whether or not the landlord provides furniture. When the original Act of Parliament giving security of tenure was introduced in 1915 furnished tenancies were excluded. However the legislation has been altered many times since then. The distinction between furnished and unfurnished lettings lost virtually all legal significance after the passing of the Rent Act 1977. Despite that a fair number of people still believe that someone cannot be a "sitting tenant" because the landlord provides furniture.

The landlord's decision whether or not to furnish the property will depend largely on the sort of tenant he is aiming for. Tenants who are entering into a three year contract are much more likely to be willing to provide their own furniture than ones who will only be there for six months. Tenants do not generally expect the furniture provided by the landlord to be of the highest quality. Furniture bought from second hand shops is usually acceptable. If the landlord who has lived in the property himself leaves, that furniture he does not want to move to his new home that should form the nucleus of what he provides for the tenants. If he does let a property as furnished, the following would be an absolute minimum of furniture he could provide:

- Sofa and armchair in the living room;
- Cabinet or sideboard of some sort;
- Kitchen table and chairs;
- Cooker;
- Refrigerator;
- Bed, wardrobe and bedside cabinet in each bedroom; and

●For students, a desk and chair in each bedroom

Large rooms will require more furniture.

Tenants generally expect even unfurnished properties to come with carpets, curtains and shelving. Supplying a washing machine, tumble drier and dish washer will make the property more attractive to tenants, but it should be remembered such machines do break down, particularly with the rough handling tenants may subject them to. Most tenants prefer to provide their own television and video. If the landlord does supply electrical equipment he is able to disclaim any responsibility for repairing it if it breaks down, but this should be pointed out clearly when the tenancy agreement is made. Sometimes the landlord will provide cutlery, crockery and bed-linen, but in respect of such personal items it would not seem unreasonable to expect all but the most impecunious tenants to supply their own. Cooking utensils such as saucepans and frying pans are normally provided by the landlord where there is a furnished tenancy. Light bulbs are strictly speaking the landlord's responsibility whether the tenancy is furnished or not. It has been known for tenants to ask landlords to pay for washing up liquid and toilet paper: only the most generous comply!

Services

If the tenancy agreement is such that the landlord has responsibility for electricity and gas bills, this will not affect the legal nature of the tenancy. Of course such an arrangement would not be attractive to most landlords if it could be avoided. The temptation on the tenants to use more heating than they really needed, knowing someone else was paying for it, might prove irresistible. However properties are sometimes situated in a block of flats with central boilers and the owners of those flats pay a flat fee service charge for their heating. In that case it is often easier for the landlord to settle the bill for this and reflect the fact in the amount of rent charged for the flat.

Sometimes the landlord will elect to provide the tenant with more personal forms of services, such as cleaning and changing the beds and even cooking meals. It may be that these would have the effect that the tenant is granted a licence rather than a lease. If these services are provided when the tenant lives in the same house as the landlord, it will for practical purposes not be a tenancy in any case (see pages 22 to 23). If the landlord is employing someone to provide these services as in a hostel, the question whether or not there is a tenancy will depend upon whether or not the tenant has *exclusive possession* of any property. If the landlord's employee visits the room daily to clean it, then the tenant may not have that degree of exclusivity. If there is not a tenancy, the tenant (strictly then, *licensee*)'s rights are considerably eradicated. This is a somewhat grey area of the law and it would be most inadvisable for a landlord to provide services purely in the belief that doing so would prevent there from being a tenancy.

Repairs

The landlord's basic repairing obligations in respect of the structure of the premises and the electricity, gas and water supplies were set out on page 32. In a tenancy for less than seven years the landlord remains under an duty to carry out these repairs even if the tenancy agreement has purported to put the responsibility on the tenants.

This though is the strictly speaking the limit of the landlord's repairing duties, unless he has agreed to do more. He is not for instance required to keep the property well decorated. Somewhat surprisingly, it has recently been decided by a court that there is no obligation on a landlord to ensure that the property does not become infested by cockroaches. However if poor decoration or infestation are a consequence of the landlord's failure to preform his repairing obligations, then he will be liable to make good the damage. A leaking roof often for instance results in damage being caused inside the premises. Similarly if the tenant's belongings are damaged because the landlord didn't carry out repairs, the landlord will be liable for this.

Although the law is not clear on the point, it is generally accepted that landlords are responsible for maintaining any furniture they provide. Furniture in the strict sense requires little maintenance: usually only when someone's carelessness has damaged it. However appliances such as cookers have the same standing as furniture for this purpose, and when they break down it is reasonable for the tenants to expect landlords to be responsible for repairs or replacements.

The landlord is however only liable to carry out repairs to defects he should have known about. The most obvious way for him to learn of them is by reason of the tenant's complaint. If he finds out otherwise, perhaps through his own inspection or someone else telling him, his duty to repair will then arise. Once the landlord finds out about the defects, he must remedy them within a reasonable time. What a reasonable time is will depend on the nature of the defect. Where the fault is a broken pipe or a total electrical failure, it will only be a matter of hours if that. Even where it is something less urgent, such as missing roof tiles, there can be little excuse for delaying more than a week or so. Only for major structural works, which inevitably take time to arrange, will the landlord be justified in taking longer. Tenants cannot however complain about the landlord's failure to do repairs when they have forgotten to tell him anything was wrong.

Landlords have a right to enter the property to inspect the state of repair upon giving 24 hours' written notice. this right should be exercised sparingly unless the tenants have asked the landlord to visit.

There have recently been a number of highly publicised deaths from carbon monoxide poisoning caused by defective gas installations in rented property. As a result legislation is currently under scrutiny the result of which is likely to be a requirement that landlords service all gas appliances once a year. A failure to comply will be a criminal offence, carrying sentences of imprisonment.

When property is in multiple occupation, such as where the landlord has let a number of bedsits in the same house, fire regulations have to be complied with.

Insurance

There is strictly speaking no duty on either the landlord or the tenant to insure the property. It is of course advisable for the landlord to do this: he has far more to lose than the tenant does if there is a fire or other disaster. The landlord on the other hand will have no particular interest in insuring the contents. Except for the most up-market tenancies, it is unlikely that the furniture the landlord has provided will be worth insuring. The tenant should be left to arrange his own insurance for his possessions.

A landlord letting property for the first time would be well advised to check with his insurance company. Sometime the fact that property is let may affect or even invalidate the insurance cover.

3. WHAT SHOULD BE PROVIDED

At the end of the tenancy

The lease will normally have spelt out the obligations of the tenants at the end of the lease. Under the draft tenancy on pages 103 to 105, which is fairly typical, the tenant has to:

- have kept the interior clean and tidy and in a good state of repair and decoration;
- have not caused any damage;
- have replaced anything they have broken;
- replace or pay for the repair or replacement of anything they have damaged;
- pay for the laundering of the linen;
- pay for the laundering of any curtains, blankets or similar items that they have soiled; and
- put anything they have moved back where it was originally.

Sometime leases include a right for the landlord to have the premises professionally cleaned at the tenant's expense whatever state they have been left in. So long as the tenants have cleaned the property reasonably thoroughly it would seem rather mean to insist on that. Likewise if the tenants have washed the sheets themselves, there would seem little point in insisting on them being laundered as well.

Obviously if there is any serious damage, the landlord has every right to demand that this be paid for. However most leases have an exception for fair wear and tear. The odd scratch on the furniture, tear on the wall paper and even broken plate really falls into this category. The longer the tenancy, the greater the degree of deterioration that would count as fair wear and tear.

The landlord will normally be able to recover any loss the tenants' conduct has caused by deducting it from the deposit. Of course if the tenants have "recovered" the deposit themselves by not paying the final instalment of rent the landlord will not be able to this. Many tenants, even ones who recover the deposit this way, are fundamentally honest and will pay for any damage if the landlord can persuade them that he has a fair claim. Nothing will deter tenants from acting honourably in this situation more quickly than the landlord demanding sums of money that are unrealistically high in relation to the damage. Theoretically if the tenants do not pay up, the landlord can try to sue them. In practice this course is hardly ever worthwhile.

From the Tenant's Perspective

Furniture and services

Usually tenants will not get much choice about whether or not furniture or services are supplied. It is obviously pointless for someone to apply to rent an unfurnished flat if he does not have any furniture and is not willing to buy some. If furniture is provided by the landlord and the flat is attractive enough it may still be worthwhile taking the tenancy. The fact that a tenancy is furnished does not usually result in the rent being increased greatly. If there is storage space such as a loft or a cellar the landlord's furniture can be hidden away, though it would be a good idea to seek his permission first.

In normal tenancies services such as cleaning and the changing of bed-linen are not provided. If the tenant is living in a hostel he is far more likely to receive them. Frequently the provision of such services has the effect that he is not granted a tenancy at all. In a hostel that probably makes very little practical difference to the tenant.

Repairs

If a landlord does not carry out repairs, the tenants have a right to deduct the costs of doing them themselves from the rent. Obviously if the tenants do adopt that course, they should keep receipts for all the monies spent. Alternatively, they could carry on paying the rent and sue the landlord for their costs of carrying out the repairs. Such a course would have little to commend it. Suing anybody is time-consuming, stressful and often very expensive. It is much better to put the defaulting landlord in the position where if anybody sues it will have to be him. Of course if the tenancy is one that the landlord is entitled to end and the tenants stop paying rent for any reason, he may well try to get rid of them. He will however have to obtain a court order before he can force the tenants to leave (see pages 84 to 85). If the repairs are major and the tenants do not want to pay for them themselves, it is also possible to obtain a court order requiring the landlord to do them (see page 98.)

If the landlord is in breach of his repairing obligations for a long time, the tenant may become entitled to damages over and above the cost of the repairs. These will be to compensate for unpleasantness of living in a home which is in a serious state of disrepair. Obviously the amount awarded will depend on the extent of the disrepair and the length of time it persists after the landlord had become aware of it. A damp patch on a bedroom wall for a few months might be worth only £100, whereas awards well over £5,000 have been made where there has been a failure to provide heating or hot water over several years. The amount of rent the tenant pays may also have a bearing on the amount of damages: the higher the rent, the higher the damages.

In some circumstances the local authority will be prepared to intervene to compel a landlord to carry out repairs. The local environmental health officer can advise on whether he considers it appropriate for the authority to become involved.

With common sense and co-operation neither landlord or tenant should have to have recourse to these legal rules. When tenants move into premises landlords are often prepared to pay for the materials to enable them to redecorate so long as the tenants are willing to carry out the work themselves. This seems a sensible arrangement from both sides. The landlord gets his property redecorated cheaply,: the tenants get to chose the decor they have to live with. Understandably some landlords are not so enthusiastic about this arrangement if the tenants show a preference for purple walls with orange ceilings: a colour scheme not so distinctive that it might deter future tenants is a reasonable requirement!

Whatever the strict legal position if essential electrical items, such as a cooker or a fridge break down, most landlords are willing to pay for their repair or replacement. If the landlord asks the tenant to arrange such repairs or replacement himself, the tenant should co-operate. Particularly for replacements a maximum price should be agreed in advance. Normally the best way for the landlord to repay the tenant is to simply accept a reduced rent for the next instalment or however long it takes to cover the cost. If the rent is being paid by standing order, then the landlord can simply reimburse the tenant by paying the money to him.

4. FINDING A TENANT OR A LANDLORD

From the Landlord's Perspective

Agents

Before taking any steps to find tenants the landlord needs to decide whether or not to use an agent, both in finding tenants and in subsequently managing the premises. The advantages of using an agent are obvious: they "know the ropes", they are likely to already have tenants on their books. Some but not all will check references. They should be able to give advice on a realistic level of rent. They will draw up the tenancy agreement and should be able to do it in such a way as to avoid the disaster of giving the tenant the permanent right to stay in the property.

Some agencies offer a guaranteed income even if the tenant defaults on the rent. Agencies who make offers of this sort should immediately arouse suspicions. It may not prove any easier to enforce such a promise than it is to enforce the tenant's promise to pay rent. If the promise is made in the name of a limited company, it will only be enforceable against the company, which will often turn out to have no assets. The owner of the company will not be personally liable. Some agencies insist on the rent being paid by the tenant to them rather than directly to the landlord. Agencies have a legitimate interest in protecting their fees and cannot be entirely blamed for doing this. However the danger is that if the agency gets into financial difficulties the landlord may end up losing rent that was held by the agent. It would be inadvisable to agree to such an arrangement with any but the longest established companies.

Landlords do sometimes use solicitors to draw up tenancy agreements for them. This shouldn't be necessary, but mistakes can be made both by landlords acting for themselves and agents. Instructing a solicitor to do this work should be safer, but of course even solicitors can make mistakes. Any adviser, whether an agent or a solicitor, who makes a costly mistake in drawing up a tenancy agreement, such as failing to serve a notice saying it is

44

to be an assured shorthold tenancy, will be liable to make up the loss suffered by the landlord. In practice enforcing such a claim is never easy. The landlord should double check that his advisers have done everything necessary before putting his signature to the tenancy agreement or allowing the tenant to start living at the premises.

If agents are appointed to manage the property, it should be agreed in writing what exactly constitutes management. The following are matters that agents often look after:

- transferring utility bills and the council tax into the name of the tenant;
- the arrangement of repairs;
- paying for repairs (agents will normally only agree to do this if the rent is being paid directly to them and they are authorised to deduct these costs from it);
- chasing the tenants if they fall into rent arrears;
- serving notices of intention to seek possession if the landlord instructs them to (agents should not commence court proceedings except through a solicitor);
- visiting the property at regular intervals (the frequency of which should be specified) to check that the tenants are not causing any damage;
- dealing with any complaints that may be made by, for instance, neighbours;
- banking the rental receipts if the landlord is abroad; and
- dealing with the council's housing benefit department, if it proves necessary.

The agent's management fee might be 10-15% of the rent. If agents arrange repairs, it is unlikely that they will negotiate to get the best deal from tradesmen the way a property owner paying with his own money might.

It is illegal for agencies to charge tenants for merely giving out landlord's addresses. Doing so is a criminal offence under the Accommodation Agencies Act 1953, although very few prosecutions are brought. Most agents in any case charge the landlord rather than the tenant.

Fees vary and it is worth shopping around. For finding tenants 10% of the rent charged over the term of the tenancy would be fairly typical.

Some agents, rather than charging a percentage of the total rent charge say three weeks' or a month's rent. This scale for payment is more likely to be attractive to a landlord who is letting the property for a long term. Sometimes extra charges are made for providing the written lease and, if used, notice of assured shorthold tenancy and for checking references. A management service is likely to be around an extra 5%. Some agents include a clause in their terms that if a tenant they have introduced subsequently buys the property they are entitled to the same interest as estate agents would have got, perhaps 2% of the purchase price.

An agent should view the premises so that he can fairly describe it to any interested tenants, but some merely take details from the landlord. Some agents are prepared to show the property to prospective tenants if the landlord wants them to, others will merely arrange appointments for the landlord to do this.

A landlord considering instructing an agent should check whether the agent intends to advertise the property or merely wait for prospective tenants to walk through his door. If the agent has offices on a busy street and a sign that make it clear he is a lettings agent, the latter will be a perfectly good way of attracting customers, though the saving in advertising costs should be reflected in the agent's prices.

Advertisements

The classified ad's column of local newspapers are usually a good means of attracting tenants. Such papers will be looked at by most people seeking a property to rent in that area and the charges are fairly small, a three line advert in a local newspaper around London would be around £6, elsewhere slightly less. The London *Evening Standard* is considerably more expensive, about £25 for the same advert, but extremely effective for property reasonably close to central London. National newspapers also carry such adverts in regionally distributed sections. The *Guardian*, for instance, currently only charges £6 for a three line advert covering the London area.

LOOT, (0171 328 1771) which is a newspaper that consists of nothing but adverts which can be placed free over the phone or in writing, is distributed throughout London and the home counties. It contains a substantial property section, is published daily and currently costs £1-10. *To Let* (0171 924 6593) claims to be London's biggest selling property paper. It provides space free to private advertisers and to agencies for on a payment of £10 per month regardless of the number of adverts. Published weekly, it costs £1. *London Lettings* (0181 445 4100) also costs £1 and is distributed in Greater London. It accepts adverts on an "premium rate" number, the charges for which can often be more than for placing the advert in the local paper. Capital Radio (0171 388 5153) runs a free flat share list, which is directed at people looking to share flats and houses rather than landlords renting property.

Free ad papers now also exist in Liverpool, Manchester, Nottingham, Derby and Leicester. Other local radio stations may be prepared to provide information about available lettings. Often tenants can be found simply by placing a card in a shop window. Most colleges keep lists of accommodation available to students and will be pleased to include any new property without charge. Many college accommodation offices will be able to provide information about realistic rent levels, although their primary interest should be in helping students rather than landlords.

Where rates are by the line, abbreviations are the order of the day.

The following is a real advert from the Evening Standard:
SW13 beaut res area grd flr dbl bdrm lg gch bth/shwr rm small k wm ideal prof cple.
Although this was more decipherable than many, what "wm" means is a complete mystery. Most prospective tenants would have no idea what it is.

Such a detailed description- abbreviated or otherwise- is in any case fairly pointless. People want to know the area, size and price. If these meet their criteria they will ring up and find out more details.

Another advert from the same edition this advert was probably just as effective although a quarter of the length and price:
N16 1 bd unfurn £110 pw

Some papers now refuse to accept abbreviations at all.

Going back to Mrs Healey's flat, which was fully described on page 12 a reasonable description to give in an advertisement might be:
E15 4 bedroom flat, lounge, close tube, shops, separate bath and toilet £180 per week, tel 081 123 4567
Abbreviated to appear in the *Evening Standard*, this would read:

E15 4b/r, 1l/r, close LT, sep btr w.c. £180 pw 081 123 4567

Local authorities and housing associations

Some local authorities also take tenancies of privately owned properties. These are then let to individuals whom the council is under a duty to house. The local authority usually requires a tenancy of at least two years. In return it will guarantee the rent throughout the period and carry out repairs and redecoration at the end of the term. Some authorities now carry out letting of this sort through housing associations. In London authorities now sometimes even take properties on this basis in neighbouring boroughs as well as within their own boundaries. People occupying properties sub-let by local authorities in this way often have problems. A landlord prepared to let in this way may therefore feel that doing so is socially responsible and desirable. The starting point for letting to a local authority would be to phone the housing department of the council in question.

Showing the property

Once the landlord has received a response to his advertisement the next stage is to make arrangements for people to view the property. If he is not living there himself and has to make a special visit to the property, there is no reason why he should not make all the appointments on the same day. He should try to keep appointments a reasonable distance of time apart. It is not in anyone's interests to have more than one group of people looking at a property at the same time. Prospective tenants tend to be a lot more reliable about turning up on time than people who are considering buying a property. If either party has to cancel an appointment, then it is common courtesy to do all he can to let the other know. This cannot be emphasised too much when someone has to make a special journey for that appointment.

If tenants like the property and the landlord likes the tenants, there is obviously no reason why it should not be let there and then. This is much easier to accomplish if the landlord has already prepared a draft agreement and any notices relevant to the tenancy. It is vital for the landlord to remember to hand over and obtain a receipt for the notices before signing the tenancy agreement or accepting any money (see pages 20 to 21). Unless the landlord is completely convinced of the tenants' respectability, accepting a cheque at this stage may be risky. Certainly the keys should not be handed over until the cheque has cleared. Even if it bounces before the tenants move in, there is still a tenancy agreement and although the legal position is not entirely clear, the tenants might be entitled to live there.

From the Tenant's Perspective

Advertisements, agents and viewing

The sources of advertisements people might use when looking for a property to live in are of course the same as those landlords will use. Some of the sources discussed on page 70 in relation to lettings in the landlord's own home may also yield property that is to be let separately. Prospective tenants sometimes try advertising their own needs. Although this may not be a particularly reliable way of finding a home, there is always a possibility that a landlord will see the advert and respond to it rather than putting his own in. Placing such an advert in a free ad's paper or a local newspaper, where the fee for a couple of lines is unlikely to be more than a few pounds, is a reasonable investment.

Beware of any agent that asks for a fee in advance or indeed that intends to charge tenants at all. Often estate agents who do not advertise the fact that they deal with lettings will be of assistance in finding rented property. Even if they do not have anything suitable on their own books, they are likely to know of other local agents who do.

When viewing property prospective tenants should come armed with documents that prove their respectability (see pages 27 to 29) and sufficient cash to pay the first month's rent and any reasonable deposit the landlord may ask for. If a property is in heavy demand, "first come, first served" is likely to apply and being there with everything the landlord is likely to require is the best way of getting to the head of the queue.

5. THE RENT

From the Landlord's Perspective

Payment of Rent

The landlord and tenant should agree as to how the rent is to be paid before the lease is completed. Some landlords like to physically collect the rent. This gives them an opportunity to visit the premises regularly and check that all is well. Doing this can be quite an effective method of ensuring that the tenant pays on time. It is much easier to "forget" to put money in the post than to find an excuse to not hand it over when actually faced with the landlord.

Probably the most reliable method of ensuring that the tenant complies with his obligations is to have him complete a standing order. This is an instruction to his bank to regularly pay a certain amount of money into the landlord's bank account. A form on which this can be done will be provided by most banks though landlords can draw up their own. The account out of which the tenant pays the rent will have to be a current account. Most deposit accounts do not have any facility for standing orders. Bank account numbers and sort codes are set out on cheque books and statements.

> **Mrs Healey prepared such a form in anticipation of finding a suitable tenant. She wrote in the details of her own bank account and left the tenant's details to be completed when she found people she wanted to let the property to:**
> **To the Manager,**
> [*Name and address of tenant's bank*],
> **Please pay £180 every Monday from my account held at your branch, no. [*number of tenant's account*] to the credit of account no. 03 67 89 12345678 held in the name of Mrs A H Healey, at Barclay's Bank, 55 High Road, St Albans, Herts (sort code 03 67 89).**
> **Signed................tenant**

The landlord should have the tenant complete and sign the form. It is then advisable for the landlord to send it to the tenant's bank rather than relying on the tenant to do so himself. (Direct debits which are similar to, and often confused with, standing orders are not appropriate for use by private landlords. They enable one person to take money directly out of another's bank account. The banks understandably restrict the right to do this to large organisations.)

If the landlord does want to collect his rent by standing order, it is advisable to have the tenant complete the standing order form when the lease is signed and perhaps to even stipulate in the lease that the rent is to be paid in this way. As with any other term of a lease, it becomes much harder for a landlord to insist upon once the tenant is installed in the property.

Raising the rent: tenancies granted after 14 January 1989

If a tenancy is granted for a specific term, the rent will remain the same throughout that term unless the lease has specified circumstances in which it can be increased. Once that term has expired the landlord can try to set a new rent. If the tenancy is a weekly or monthly one, the landlord cannot attempt to increase the rent until after the tenancy has run for at least a year.

There are also procedural restrictions on the landlord's ability to increase the rent. The landlord must serve a notice of increase. This must give the tenant at least one month's warning of the increase. If rent is paid quarterly, three months' notice has to be given; if yearly, six months' notice. The notice must be in the official form a copy of which appears on page 110. If there is more than one tenant, it must be addressed to both or all of them. If the landlord wants to alter any other terms of the tenancy, perhaps converting an unfurnished tenancy into a furnished one then he must also serve a notice. This is similar to the one in respect of a rent increase and likewise gives the tenants an opportunity to accept or reject the change.

The tenant on receiving a notice of increase can apply to a *rent assessment committee* to determine the rent. This rent will be based on what a reasonable market rent for the property would be. If there is a scarcity of rented property in the area, that will be taken into account. What the rent assessment committee will not do is allow a landlord to charge an exorbitant rent to a tenant who is desperate to carry on living in the same home when no-one else would be willing to pay such a high price. When an application is made to a rent assessment committee it will usually arrange for its members- normally there are three of them one of whom is a lawyer- to inspect the property. Then there will be a hearing when the landlord and tenant can advance any arguments about the proper level of rent. Occasionally this hearing may take place before the inspection.

In practice many, perhaps most, landlords simply ignore the notice requirement and tell the tenant informally that they are increasing the rent. So long as there is a reasonably amicable relationship between the landlord and the tenant there is little to be gained with complying with the legal formalities. However if the landlord and tenant fall out it is the landlord who will suffer problems. Unless there has been some sort of formal agreement to increase the rent, the tenant cannot be compelled to pay the increased rent.

Raising the rent: assured shorthold tenancies

The same rules as to initial rents and as to increasing them apply to assured shorthold tenancies as they do to ordinary assured tenancies discussed above. However with an assured shorthold tenancy the tenant does have an initial right to apply to a rent assessment committee to alter the rent agreed between him and the landlord. The circumstances in which the committee can interfere with the rent are very limited. It will only do so if it believes that the landlord is charging a rent which is significantly higher than the landlord might have been expected to obtain having regard to rents charged for similar properties in the same location. Such an application is made by the tenant obtaining and sending to the committee a prescribed form, blank copies of which can be obtained from law stationers or rent officers.

If a rent is set using this procedure, the landlord cannot attempt to raise it again for a year. However if the term of the tenancy expires he may obtain possession against the tenant. There is nothing to stop a landlord from then granting a new tenancy to someone else at the old rent, assuming of course he can find anyone willing to pay it.

Raising the rent: tenancies granted before 15 January 1989

Strictly speaking in the case of tenancies granted before 15 January 1989 the landlord has no right to increase the rent except by applying to the rent officer for a *fair rent*. Fair rents generally are discussed in the tenant's section below. As fair rents are considerably below market rents, the landlord may find that applying for a fair rent will actually result in the rent decreasing. Even once an increased rent has been assessed, the landlord can only implement it by serving a notice of increase on the tenant.

The landlord can ask the tenant to agree to an increased rent without applying to the rent officer. An agreement reached this way will only be binding if it is written and signed by the landlord and the tenant and it contains a amongst other things a statement that the tenant is entitled to apply for a fair rent.

The rent book

If a landlord collects a rent, rather than having it paid by standing order, it is a good idea to provide the tenant with a rent book, and to sign it every time rent is paid. Where the rent is paid weekly, provision of a rent book is a legal requirement, and there is certain information that has to be stated in the book. Books in the correct form can be obtained from many general or legal stationers.

From the Tenant's Perspective

Tenancies granted after 14 January 1989

The landlord's obligation to serve the appropriate notice to an assured tenant before increasing the rent is discussed under the same heading in the landlord's section. If the landlord tries to increase the rent without serving a notice the tenant has to decide whether or not to pay it. If the increase is an unreasonable one, particularly if it is to a level the tenant would rather quit the property than pay, the tenant should simply carry on paying the old rent. If on the other hand the increase is reasonable, perhaps equivalent to no more than the rate of inflation, there is probably little to be gained by refusing to pay it. Doing so will antagonise the landlord. If he is entitled to, the landlord may well apply for a possession order. It is easy enough for him to serve a proper notice of increase. A tenant who pays an increase when the landlord hasn't gone through the proper procedure may find himself able to eventually get the money back. This rather sneaky course would not have been available had the tenant taken advantage of the landlord's failure straight away: all he would have done is drive the landlord into following the correct procedure.

Tenancies granted before 15 January 1989

In the case of tenancies first granted before 15 January 1989, even ones that have been subsequently renewed, the tenant has considerably greater rights to apply for a registered rent. This right is much more draconian than those discussed above in relation to assured and assured shortholds. The application is made to a *rent officer* rather than a rent assessment committee. It has to be on the official form which can be obtained from the rent officer. This asks about the property and also requires the tenant to say what he thinks the fair rent should be. Specifying a sum considerably less than the present rent is probably the best course. Once the application is made, the rent officer will send a form asking the landlord to provide certain information. The rent officer than inspects the premises and will if either party has requested it arrange a meeting between himself the landlord and the tenant. He will then decide upon the rent to be registered. The landlord and the tenant both have a right of appeal to a rent assessment committee if dissatisfied with his decision.

The landlord cannot compel the tenant to agree to any increase in rent without the rent first being referred to a rent officer. In the case of pre 15 January 1989 tenancies the tenant is usually in a very strong position to resist any increase the landlord wants to impose unless there is already a fair rent.

Once a fair rent is assessed the landlord is not entitled to recover any more rent than that assessed. In the unlikely event of the fair rent being more than is currently paid, the landlord is not immediately entitled to increase the rent. He can only do so once the term of the contract has expired.

To give an example of this: suppose 41c Wilson Road has been let since 1 July 1987 by Mrs Benn to Mr Foot. This has been renewed every year. The rent payable from 1 July 1994 was £100 per week. Mr Foot applies for a registered rent and one is determined on 31 March 1995 at £75 per week. From 1 April onwards Mr Foot will only have to pay that amount. On the other hand had the rent

been raised to £110 per week, Mrs Healey could only charge £100 per week until the expiry of the lease on 30 June 1995. Then she could recover the higher rent but would first have to serve a notice of increase. Mr Foot would be entitled to leave the premises if he did not wish to pay the higher rent. In any case Mrs Healey is entitled to agree to take a lower rent. However even if he enters into another agreement to pay a rent higher than that registered Mr Foot could not be compelled to pay it. Indeed if he pays a higher rent, he is entitled to sue to recover it for two years after he has paid it.

Registered rents are almost always less than the rent agreed between the landlord and the tenant. There is no specific formula used by rent officers, but they have to disregard any increase of value caused by a scarcity of rented property in the vicinity. The best way to find out what a registered rent on a particular property is likely to be is to examine the register kept by the rent officer. From this it will be possible to compare rents recently set on similar properties. It is important to remember to check the date on any assessment: one made several years ago will have little relevance to a new application.

6. TAX AND HOUSING BENEFIT

From the Landlord's Perspective

Income tax

The rent received by a landlord is treated as his income for tax purposes. The basis upon which it is assessed depends to an extent upon whether the property let is furnished or unfurnished. There are some differences in the way that furnished and unfurnished premises are actually taxed but these are unlikely to have any practical effect on the small landlord. If the landlord provides meals and services for a number of tenants, the resulting income may be treated as coming from a trade rather than property. Again this will not have a great practical impact on the amount of tax payable, but the landlord may be able to persuade the Revenue to allow him a greater range of deductions from his income.

Payment of rent directly to the Inland Revenue

An agent who receives rent can be required by the Inland Revenue to pay a proportion to the Revenue rather than to the landlord on account of the landlord's tax liability. A direction to this effect is likely to be made where the landlord has previously defaulted on payments. An agent who does not comply with such a direction can be personally liable for the lost tax as well as having to pay a fine.

If the landlord lives abroad, the tenant, is under an obligation to deduct basic rate income tax from the rent and pay it directly to the Inland Revenue.

6. TAX AND HOUSING BENEFIT

Exemptions from tax

Where the landlord lets rooms in his own home a certain amount of rent-currently £3,250 per year- is exempt from taxation. If there is more than one landlord, perhaps the couple who own the house, they can either share this allowance or have it allocated to one of them. They cannot however both claim the full amount. Also where this exemption is claimed the landlord will not be able to deduct any expenses either on the £3,250 itself or any surplus which is subject to tax. Where a person obtains an income substantially in excess of this amount from renting rooms at his home he should seek the advice of an accountant as to whether or not it is in his interests to claim the allowance.

Deductions from tax

Expenditure on the property can be deducted from rental income to give the figure on which tax is paid. The following matters are all accepted by the Inland Revenue as being proper matters for deduction:

- insuring the property;
- repairs and maintenance;
- agents' fees or commission;
- water rates;
- council tax;
- rent paid to a superior landlord (most usually ground rent and/or service charges payable under a long lease);
- legal fees; and
- interest paid on loans secured on the property, i.e. mortgages, although there are exceptions to this entitlement.

Improvements, as opposed to repairs, carried out on the property are not deductible. In practice the Revenue is unlikely to enquire too closely about the nature of work carried out unless an enormous allowance is claimed.

Stamp duty

Stamp duty is payable on leases. For furnished tenancies lasting less than a year this is merely a nominal sum of £1. Otherwise it is normally 1% of the annual rent. There is however strictly speaking no obligation to pay this duty. The only sanction for non-payment is that a court should refuse to receive an unstamped document in evidence. If a dispute arises which looks likely to lead to court proceedings the landlord should then consider stamping the lease. A penalty may be levied for late payment, but the fear of this is not generally enough to encourage landlords of short term tenancies to pay it in advance. In practice courts frequently overlook the rule about not looking at unstamped leases.

Payment of housing benefit directly to the landlord

Housing benefit is essentially a payment made to the tenant rather than the landlord. Local authorities are though under a duty to prevent its abuse. It is therefore possible to arrange for the local authority paying the benefit to do so directly to the landlord. The local authority must agree to do this where there are eight weeks' arrears of rents, unless it would be in the interests of the tenant not to do this. This exception is likely to apply where the tenant states that he has a substantial claim against the landlord for disrepair or harassment. Where the exception does apply, the local authority withholds payment altogether rather than paying it to the tenant. If there is an arrears problem and the landlord believes the tenant is receiving housing benefit, he should contact the housing benefit department of the local authority to arrange direct payment.

Housing benefit and possession for arrears of rent

Often problems in obtaining housing benefit cause tenants to get into difficulties with paying their rent. If a landlord has let a property knowing that the tenant is going to claim housing benefit, then it is probably best for him to wait while the local authority sorts matters out. If the arrears are accruing through no fault of the tenant's, it is unlikely that the court would exercise any discretion in the landlord's favour. Once there are three months' arrears of rent and Ground 8 applies (see page 75) the court would have to order possession regardless of any fault by the housing benefit authorities.

If on the other hand the tenant had taken on a tenancy on the implicit understanding that he was going to pay the rent himself, but then immediately applies for housing benefit, the court is much more likely to sympathise with the landlord. An intermediate situation might be the case of a longstanding tenant who has paid his rent reliably but who needs to apply for housing benefit because, for instance, he has lost his job.

From the Tenant's Perspective

Payment of rent directly to the Inland Revenue

The tenant is obliged to pay a proportion of the rent directly to the Inland Revenue where the landlord lives abroad. This is not dependent upon there having been any previous default by the landlord. Where the landlord does live abroad, the tenants would be advised to contact the local tax office as soon as they move in to establish the position in relation to this. A landlord who envisaged being paid the full amount directly is unlikely to be very pleased by the tenants paying his tax for him. There is in practice little that can be done about this. If the tenants do not co-operate with the Inland Revenue, they may well find themselves personally liable to pay the landlord's tax!

Eligibility for housing benefit

Housing benefit is a state payment to tenants on low incomes to assist them with their rent payments. Those in receipt of income support should receive the entire amount of the rent. Students are in almost all cases disqualified from receiving housing benefit.

Backdated claims

Tenants are entitled to claim housing benefit to cover a period one year back from the date they made the claim. For this to be done the tenant must show good cause for not having made the claim earlier. This is interpreted liberally by many authorities and a simple nonawareness of entitlement will often be sufficient.

Excessive rent

If the local authority believes the rent is excessive for the type of property or where the property is grander than the tenant reasonably needs, it may reduce the amount of housing benefit it pays to what it considers an appropriate amount. If a fair rent or registered rent has been assessed in respect of the property, the local authority will not pay a greater amount than that. The authority cannot exercise the power on the basis of the accommodation being more than the tenant reasonably needs during the first three months the tenant claims, if the tenant had previously been paying the rent himself. There is in turn an exception to that exception if the tenant had been eligible for housing benefit in the last year. There are restrictions on exercising the power where the tenant is a pensioner, unable to work through illness or has children under 19. Rules in relation to payment of housing benefit for high rents are likely to be reviewed in 1995.

If housing benefit is reduced under this power, the reduction will be equivalent to the proportion by which the local authority believes too much rent is being paid.

Suppose a tenant is paying a rent of £100 per week, but the local authority only believes it should be £75. The tenant's income is such that he is entitled to have half his rent paid by the housing benefit authorities. With the deduction he would have £37-50 paid rather than £50.

Housing benefit is only intended to cover the rent itself and not ancillary matters which may be included in the payment described as rent. Therefore if the landlord pays the water rates, provides heating, pays the utility bills, provides services or meals, the amount of housing benefit will be adjusted to deduct these things. However if the landlord waives rent for a period up to eight weeks because the tenant has carried out repairs or redecoration, housing benefit will still be paid during that period.

Payment of housing benefit

Housing benefit should be paid within 14 days of the authority receiving a valid claim. In practice it often takes a lot longer to process applications. A tenant finding himself in a position where the landlord is threatening legal action because of arrears which have built up due to non-payment of housing benefit should instruct a solicitor who would then put pressure on the local authority to pay the arrears. The effect of the weight of this as an excuse in possession claims is discussed on page 58 to 59.

There is no legal obligation on a tenant who receives housing benefit to hand it over to his landlord. Of course if he does not do so, the landlord can sue him, but it will be arrears of rent that he is sued for not the housing benefit. A criminal prosecution alleging theft against a tenant who retained housing benefit failed for this reason.

7. TRANSFERRING A TENANCY

From the Landlord's Perspective

Transfers to a new tenant

Generally speaking residential tenancies whenever granted cannot be transferred from one tenant to another. If the tenant moves out and purports to transfer the tenancy to another person, the landlord should have no difficulty in obtaining a possession order. The new occupant will not be a protected, statutory or assured tenant and hence will have no statutory protection. Where a tenancy was granted after 14 January 1989 and the landlord had charged a *premium*, then this rule does not apply unless the agreement contained a term which specifically prohibits *subletting* or *assigning* the tenancy. A premium can include, for instance, any payment towards the landlord's costs of preparing the tenancy agreement and a deposit in excess of two months' rent. If the landlord appointed an agent to let the property and some or all of the agent's fees were paid by the tenant, this can constitute a premium.

Death of the landlord

Generally speaking the death of the landlord has less effect on the tenancy than that of the tenant. The tenancy continues. However most of the rights that the landlord had will pass to his estate. These rights will be exercised by his *personal representatives*, also known as *executors* (if he made a will) and his *administrators* (if he did not). These are the people with responsibility for sorting out the landlord's affairs. They are not necessarily the same people who will actually be entitled to the landlord's property, who are *beneficiaries*. Often the personal representatives are professional advisers such as solicitors or a bank. They however have to act in the best interests of the beneficiaries. It sometimes happens that tenants who have been allowed by a landlord to stay in premises very cheaply as a gesture of friendship, find themselves facing far less generous executors. Where personal representatives do act in a way that was very different from the landlord, it may be possible to make an application to the court in respect of the landlord's estate. This involves a complicated area of law outside the scope of this book and is certainly not the sort of action that can be contemplated without the help of a solicitor.

If a notice saying the tenancy is an assured shorthold has been served, the personal representatives and anyone to whom they pass the property whether it goes to a beneficiary or it is sold, will be able rely on the notice to evict the tenants. If a notice saying that the landlord could recover possession because he had lived there himself had been served and the tenancy began on or after 15 January 1989, then this will have the same wide effect after the landlord's death. On the other hand if the notice had said that the landlord intended living there some time in the future or the tenancy began before that date, it cannot be relied upon if the property is sold by the personal representatives.

If there are other grounds for possession, such as arrears of rent, executors or anyone else to whom the property passes are in exactly the same position as the original landlord.

Where the tenant had been sharing accommodation with the landlord and hence had no statutory protection, the position is legally complicated. In the majority of cases the tenant will only gain the benefit of statutory protection if no action has been taken by the personal representatives within two years of the landlord's death.

From the Tenant's Perspective

Death of the tenant: tenancy granted before 15 January 1989

The position when the tenant dies is complicated to say the least. Often tenancies are granted jointly to two people. In that case the survivor of them will be entitled to carry on as the sole tenant.

There are intricate statutory rules to decide when and if another person who was previously not a tenant, is entitled to succeed on the death of a tenant.

Where the tenancy was originally granted before 15 January 1989 the following rules apply:

- the surviving spouse of a tenant has an automatic right to carry on living there regardless of whether or not the tenancy was in joint names. This right however only applies so long as the spouse was living at the property at the time of the former tenant's death;
- "spouse" includes a person who was living with the tenant as his or her husband or wife even if not legally married;
- where the tenant died without leaving a spouse any, other member of the tenant's family who had lived with him at the property for at least two years up to his death is entitled to succeed;
- "members of the family" includes children and grandchildren (whether natural, step- or adopted), parents and brothers and sisters;
- homosexual couples and platonic adult friends will not be treated as "members of the family";
- if there is more than one family member living with the tenant at the time of his death, they can agree which is to become the tenant. If they cannot agree, they can apply to the court for a decision as to which has the best entitlement;
- where the surviving spouse has succeeded to the tenancy, the new tenancy will be treated as if it had been granted before 15 January 1989 except that succession will only be possible by someone who had been living at the property with both the original tenant and the successor for the two years up to their respective deaths; and
- where a member of the family other than the spouse succeeds, he will only become an assured tenant and the resulting tenancy will be treated like any other granted after 14 January 1989 but without any right to a further succession.

To give an example: Mr and Mrs Jenkins had been granted a joint tenancy in 1978. Mr Jenkins died in 1983. In 1985 Mrs Jenkins met a Mr Crossman. In that year he and his, then 13 year old, daughter, Barbara Crossman, moved into the property, where he co-habited with Mrs Jenkins. Mrs Jenkins died in 1990. Mr Crossman died in 1992. Barbara, who had continued living in the property, married in 1994. In 1995 Barbara dies. Is her husband entitled to the tenancy?

The first issue is, do the pre-1989 rules apply? The answer to that is yes: it is the date of the original tenancy not of any subsequent succession that is crucial.

Then, was Mrs Jenkins entitled to succeed Mr Jenkins? Clearly she was and as they were joint tenants it was not strictly speaking a succession, so she became a tenant in her own right.

Then, was Mr Crossman entitled to succeed Mrs Jenkins? Yes, so long as they had lived together as husband and wife for he would be treated as her spouse. This was the first succession.

Then, was Barbara entitled to succeed Mr Crossman? Probably, she was his daughter and hence a member of his family. She had been living with him at the property for more than two years. Being Mrs Jenkins' step-daughter she was also a member of her family and had been living with her as such for the two years up to her death. This was the second succession.

There are two reasons why Barbara's husband would not be entitled to succeed. Firstly, only two successions are allowed. Secondly, he had never been a member of the original tenant, Mrs Jenkins' family. The fact that he had lived in the property less than two years would not of itself prevent him succeeding, although it would have done had he been anyone other than a spouse.

Death of the tenant: tenancy granted after 14 January 1989

The only basis on which there can be succession to an assured tenancy is where the tenant's spouse was living with him at the property the time of his death. "Spouse" again includes a person who was living as husband or wife with the tenant without being legally married. There can only be one succession under these rules. Therefore if a person dies and is succeeded to the tenancy by his wife and she remarries, the new husband will never be entitled to succeed. If however the tenancy had originally been granted to the husband and wife jointly, there will not be a succession when the wife becomes the sole tenant on the husband's death. Then the new husband would be entitled to succeed, but would not be able in turn to pass the tenancy onto any new wife he may acquire.

Bankruptcy

If the tenant himself goes bankrupt that is unlikely to have much effect on the tenancy. The tenancy will probably not be an asset of much interest to his creditors. When a person goes bankrupt leases that he owns *vests* in his *trustee-in-bankruptcy*. If the tenancy involves the payment of a very substantial rent ,it is possible that the trustee might disclaim it, which would entitle the landlord to immediate possession. If the term of the tenancy has expired, there will be a statutory tenancy and this will not vest in the trustee. A bankrupt tenant may be able to get housing benefit (see pages 59 to 61).

The landlord's bankruptcy is likely to have a greater practical impact. The landlord's interest likewise becomes vested in the trustee-in-bankruptcy, whose duty it is to obtain as much money as he can for the creditors. The trustee will be able to take advantage of any basis on which the landlord might have obtained possession. Often it will be in the creditors' interests to sell the property, if they are able to obtain possession. The resulting proceeds will be much easier to share out than a relatively small periodic rent.

Ground 2 for obtaining possession of property subject to tenancies granted after 14 January 1989 may well apply in this situation. If the landlord had served a notice before the tenancy started saying that he had or intended in the future to live there, a mortgagee will be able to rely on this Ground to obtain possession.

8. LETTING ROOMS AT HOME

From the Landlord's Perspective

The legal position of a lodger

In legal and practical terms the relationship between a home-owner and someone he allows to lodge in the property is very different from that between a landlord who lets a whole house or flat to his tenants. Lodgers are sometimes referred to as *paying guests*. This description, if slightly archaic, is also apposite. The lodger is living in someone else's home and it would obviously be very undesirable for any law to give him an entitlement to stay once the home-owner no longer wanted him. The relationship is a personal as much as a financial one and it is right that the law should have very little say in it. In a few rare cases where the lodger moved in before 15 January 1989 and has his own clearly marked territory in the property to which the landlord has very little access, there may be a *restricted contract*. This has the effect that there may be minor restrictions on the landlord obtaining possession. These however amount to a series of procedural hoops for the landlord to go through, which might delay him, rather than a serious barrier to getting the lodger out. Where such a longstanding relationship has broken down and the tenant is not prepared to move amicably, the landlord should seek legal advice.

Whether to have a lodger

Often the decision to take a lodger is the result of the home-owner's financial need. A spare bedroom is a potential source of income. Many people feel, with considerable justification, that by letting out unused rooms they are performing a socially valuable service. Particularly for young single householders having a lodger can also be attractive as a source of company. Countless life-long friendships and more than a few marriages have grown out of such an arrangement. For others though having a lodger would amount to a discomfiting loss of privacy. For people who see it in those terms, unless the financial need is absolutely dire, it is probably best to avoid taking in lodgers. A landlord who resents sharing his home is likely to let that resentment show, with the result that there will be two people in close proximity making each other feel uncomfortable.

Generally speaking rents charged to lodgers are a little less than to tenants. To some extent the lodger is receiving a discount for having to live in somebody else's home. This slightly lower rent is largely cancelled out by the tax advantages for people who rent out rooms in their homes (see page 57).

Before taking a lodger it is advisable to check household insurance policies to ensure that the presence of a lodger is not going to effect their validity.

When considering whether to take someone as a lodger, it is as important to decide whether one could actually get on with that person as whether or not they are likely to reliable in matters such as paying rent. That is a purely subjective matter and it is worth spending a bit of time chatting to the person to establish whether there are common interests and a reasonable personal rapport before making a decision.

Reaching an agreement with the lodger

The rules which the lodger will have to respect should be established at the outset. The question of whether overnight guests are going to be allowed should be agreed upon, as should any terms banning the lodger from using certain parts of the property. It is unfair for someone to be allowed to move in and then be told that there are to be restrictions preventing him using the property as if it were his own home. Similarly if the landlord is a non-smoker and expects the lodger not smoke, this should be made clear, and lodgers who would be upset by a smoky house should make enquiries before committing themselves to living somewhere. Normally the landlord is responsible for paying bills, though the lodger will have to keep a record of and pay for any telephone calls he makes.

It is unwise for either party to commit themselves to an agreement that the lodger should stay for any set period. A month's notice on either side should be sufficient. A formal tenancy agreement is usually not appropriate for a lodger. However a letter of welcome doubling as one setting out "the rules" is a good idea: if things do turn sour, it might help each party know where they stand.

8. LETTING ROOMS AT HOME

It has already been stated that Mrs Healey would decide to rent out the spare room bedroom in Heath Cottage. A rough and ready calculation of the rent for the whole of the cottage came to £163 per week. A lodger sharing the house with just the owner might be expected to pay a little over one-third of that, perhaps £60. To find herself a lodger she placed a card in the window of the nearest shop. As she wasn't paying by the line she could afford to rather more effusive than when she was advertising 41a Wilson Road in newspapers.

ROOM TO LET

Room to let in pleasant two bedroom cottage with garden and plenty of living space. Would suit quiet young woman. Non-smoker preferred. Rent £60 per week. Telephone 0923 666666

Assuming as a result of this card she finds a person whom she wants as a lodger: Jane Rees, Mrs Healey might write to her as follows:

Dear Jane,

I am pleased that you have decided to come and live with me at Heath Cottage. The rent as discussed will be £60 per week, which you will pay me every Tuesday in advance. Either of us is entitled to end this arrangement on giving the other four weeks' notice. You will of course have your own bedroom and be free to use the rest of the house. I would however ask that you do not have any guests staying overnight or remaining here after 11 p.m. unless I have agreed to this in advance. I would also ask that you and any

guests do not smoke anywhere in the house except your own bedroom.

I would ask you to sign a copy of this letter to indicate your agreement to this.

Best wishes,

Angela Healey

Finding a lodger

Finding a lodger should be no harder than finding a tenant (see pages 44 to 48). Local newspapers have a role to play, less so perhaps agents. Some institutions are for ever searching for rooms. As well as conventional colleges, foreign language schools are a likely source of lodgers particularly in the summer. Maybe friends will know of someone looking for a room. Professional football clubs often want landlords (more usually landladies) prepared to take in their apprentices and provide meals and a quasi-parental eye.

From the Tenant's Perspective

Being a lodger

From the point of view of the lodger it has to be appreciated that there is not going to be the same degree of independence as living in a place that has been let as a separate home by a landlord. The lodger's status, is always at least in part that of a guest, who has to abide by the conventions of his host. If the landlord goes to bed at ten o'clock every night, the lodger will probably feel a little uneasy staying up and moving around the house, however quietly, until two o'clock. If the landlord and the lodger don't get on, it will inevitably be the lodger who has to go. Perhaps because of the lodger's ambiguous status rooms are usually let at rates around 25% less than would be charged for the equivalent space as a tenant on an equal footing with the other occupants.

A lodger's legal rights

The legal position is to an extent a reflection of the lodger's social position. From the point of view of the law the difference between the position of a lodger and a tenant is that a lodger has virtually no rights. If the landlord has agreed in advance to give him a month's notice or if he is allowed to live there for a specified period, then that agreement must of course be honoured. If nothing has been said about notice, the landlord still has to give a reasonable period of notice. How long this will be will depend largely on how long the lodger has been there. For one who has been there several years, a month may not be sufficient. However if only a short time has elapsed, then a shorter period may be enough. Once that has expired there is no restriction on the landlord's right to possession. Theoretically there need not even be a court order. However evicting a lodger against his will is an extremely risky process. The fact that a landlord was doing so will be no defence against an allegation of assault. Such a course should never be considered without first seeking legal advice. It is far safer to obtain a court order. There is a procedure which should enable the landlord to have obtained a possession order within a matter of weeks if not days (see pages 90 to 91). However the landlord is not entitled to start proceedings until any notice period or agreed term of the tenancy has expired.

"Flat sharing"

Unless a tenancy agreement prohibits sharing, there is no reason why a tenant established in a property cannot take a lodger rather than share the tenancy with the lodger. Sharing the tenancy requires the approval of the landlord and may mean that the newcomer has as many rights as the original tenant. If someone has been living in a place a long time, he may be unwilling to do this. Sometimes however the prospective newcomer may express a reluctance to agree to be a lodger rather than a joint tenant. A possible compromise might be to agree that the lodger should become a tenant after a trial period, if he and the original tenant are still getting along.

If a lodger is required to pay more than half the rent that the tenant is paying to the landlord, he may well understandably feel resentful. Whilst a tenant who takes such a high rent from a lodger could be accused of being greedy, there is little that can be done to prevent him from doing so.

THE LANDLORDS' AND TENANTS' HANDBOOK

Whilst the lodger's legal position may be vastly different from a tenant's the human issues of people having to live in close proximity are much the same whether one is another's lodger or there are sharing on a legally equal basis.

Sharing a property often works better when it is done by a group of strangers who have joined up for the purpose of sharing rather than a group of friends who move in together. Often people assume their friends will have the same outlook on matters as they do. However just because people find each other very good company in the pub and at college does not mean they will have the same views on how soon after eating washing up should be done. The doing of chores like the washing up, wandering around the house undressed, walking into other people's rooms without knocking, the division of bills, the playing of loud music, bolting doors at night and the unauthorised borrowing of property are just a few of the things over which people can fall out. When strangers move in together everybody tends to be on their best behaviour until all the occupants have got to know each other properly, by which time an unspoken consensus about what is and isn't acceptable has been arrived at.

Whether the house is shared with complete strangers or with people one has known since primary school, it is always better to deal with any resentments by bringing them up in good humoured way as soon as they arise, rather than let them build up until an explosive abusive row is the only way of tackling them.

9. ENDING THE TENANCY

From the Landlord's Perspective

The legal theory

It is easier to gain a practical understanding of the rules which apply to possession orders if one has a grasp of the very basic legal principles underlying them. For a landlord to obtain possession he needs to show two things:

- that the tenant no longer has a contractual right to be in possession of the premises, and;
- that one of the statutory grounds or basis for granting possession has arisen.

Where a tenancy is granted for a fixed term, the contractual right ends when that term expires. However so long as the tenant remains in possession of the property he does so as a *statutory tenant*.

If there is a forfeiture clause (see pages 33 and 34) and the tenant does something that entitles the landlord to forfeit the lease, that will end the tenant's contractual right even if the term has not expired. When this situation arises and the landlord needs to rely on a forfeiture clause for breach of a term other than for the payment of rent, he must first serve a notice on the tenant requiring him to remedy the breach. The procedure relating to such a notice is complex and drafting one is a skilled job. An account of how to do that is outside the scope of this book, and any landlord finding he needs to serve such a notice would be well advised to consult a solicitor.

Where a tenancy is not for a specific period, but merely has been renewed automatically every week or every month the landlord need not do anything more than serve the notice appropriate to the type of tenancy to end the tenant's contractual right.

Different forms of notice have to be served depending upon whether the tenancy was granted before (a protected tenancy) or after (an assured tenancy) 15 January 1989.

If the tenant is still living at the premises, the landlord will have to show that one of these statutory basis for ordering possession applies. These are different depending on whether or not the tenancy was granted after 14 January 1989.

If the tenant ceases to live in the property, it will be sufficient for the landlord to merely show he has the contractual right. The tenant's statutory protection will no longer apply and it will not be necessary for the landlord to show a statutory basis.

Often tenants are happy for the landlord to have possession but want him first to obtain a court order. If the landlord does get such an order, the tenant is then more likely to be entitled to local authority housing: if he had left voluntarily, he would be *intentionally homeless*, which would make it harder for him to be rehoused. Landlords may resent being put through the process of obtaining a possession order from the court for this reason, although there is very little they can do about it.

As a general rule courts are inclined not to make outright orders for possession when there is merely a discretion to do so. County court judges are acutely aware of the problems caused by homelessness and whilst not necessarily unsympathetic to the position of a landlord who has an unwanted tenant, consider his suffering the lesser of two evils. If there are arrears of rent, a compromise is often reached by making a *suspended possession order*. This will have the effect that a landlord will become entitled to possession only if the tenant fails to pay the rent in future. Similarly if possession is applied for on the basis of some other form of misbehaviour on the part of the tenant, the court may suspend the order on the condition that the tenant does not repeat that misconduct. There is no power to suspend the possession order when a mandatory ground for possession applies.

Grounds for possession under tenancies granted after 14 January 1989

The basis on which a court can order possession in respect of tenancies granted after 14 January 1989 are listed in Schedule 2 to the Housing Act 1988. They are known as *Grounds*. Grounds 1 to 8 are mandatory, which means if they exist and the landlord has complied with the correct procedures, the court has to make a possession order. Grounds 9 to 16 are discretionary, giving the court a choice whether or not to grant possession when they apply.

1. Non payment of rent

There are three different statutory grounds for possession based on non-payment of rent. These are:

- That the rent is at least three months in arrears both at the time of the serving of the notice that the landlord intends seeking possession (see page 83) and of the court hearing (Ground 8);
- That there are some arrears of rent both when the notice was served and at the time proceedings were commenced (Ground 10); and
- That the tenant has persistently delayed in paying rent (Ground 11).

(The exact wording of these and a number of other Grounds can be found on page 112). Ground 8 relates to a more extreme state of affairs than the other two and when it applies, the others almost certainly will too. If Ground 8 does apply, the court must order possession, whereas the other two merely give the court a discretion to do so. If an action is commenced on the basis of Ground 8, there is always a possibility that the tenant will pay off the arrears. If that does happen, the court will consider making a possession order on the basis of the other Grounds.

2. Other misbehaviour by the tenant

There are four Grounds- all discretionary- which deal with misconduct on the part of the tenant not relating to payment of rent. These are:

- The tenant has broken one or more of the conditions of the tenancy (Ground 10);
- The property has deteriorated because of the actions of the tenant or anyone living with him, (unless the tenant is taking proper steps to get rid of that person) (Ground 13);
- The tenant or anyone living with him has been guilty of conduct that has constituted a nuisance to the occupiers of adjoining property (Ground 14); and
- The condition of the furniture has deteriorated because of the actions of the tenant or anyone living with him, (unless the tenant is taking proper steps to get rid of that person) (Ground 15).

The tenant keeping pets in the property when the lease contains a prohibition on doing so is the sort of matter that is likely to lead to an application being made pursuant to Ground 10. If the lease contains terms prohibiting the tenant from causing damage or nuisance, this Ground will apply equally with 13 or 14 if the tenant does indulge in such behaviour (the Particulars of Claim on pages 93 to 94 are based on this situation). In practical terms the landlord is in no better a position because an action of the tenant offends more than one Ground. On the other hand if by separate actions, the tenant has managed to breach more than one Ground or the same Ground more than once, the court is less likely to exercise its discretion not to make a possession order.

The most frequent and obvious form of nuisance by the tenant is making too much noise. If there are complaints from neighbours that the tenant has been persistently disturbing them, then the court may well be prepared to make a possession order notwithstanding the normal reluctance to render someone homeless. On the other hand a landlord who brings an action based on one loud party is highly unlikely to succeed.

Where there is damage to the property, the court will also have regard to the degree of damage and to the tenant's willingness to make good.

3. Where the landlord has served a notice before the tenancy commenced

The situations where a landlord is entitled to serve a notice which will in some situations give him an automatic right to possession when the tenancy expires were discussed on pages 20 and 21. Leaving aside assured shorthold tenancies which will be dealt with separately, much the most important of these is Ground 1 where the landlord has lived in the premises himself or intends to do so in future. If the landlord actually has lived in the premises, then there is nothing more for him to prove to obtain possession on this Ground. If he has not lived there before, he will have to show that he (or his spouse) now requires the property as his only or principal home. With this Ground, like all the others discussed under this heading, the making of a possession order is mandatory.

If the landlord was entitled to serve a Ground 1 notice but failed to do so, then the court may if it is *just and equitable* dispense with the notice. This is most likely to be done where the landlord had told the tenant that it had been his own home or might be in future but had forgotten to actually serve a formal notice. In that situation it would be harsh to deprive the landlord of his home. On the other hand if the landlord had said nothing to the tenant about such matters, it would be unfair for the tenant to be evicted because of them. The court has the same discretion where a landlord has lost his interest to his mortgagee, which is claiming possession under Ground 2. However in that situation it is much less likely to exercise the discretion against the tenant. In the rare cases where a landlord has been entitled to serve a notice under one of the Grounds 3 to 5 there is no discretion at all to dispense with the notice.

4. Redevelopment

If the landlord wishes to demolish or carry out substantial works on the property, this will in some circumstances entitle him to possession (Ground 6). This is by far the most complicated of the statutory Grounds. Landlords considering such work should consult a solicitor to find out if this condition may apply to them as should tenants faced with a claim by a landlord for possession on this basis. Possession will only be granted if it is not practical for the tenant to remain in occupation of some or all of the property while the works are being carried on, or if he is not willing to continue living there on that basis. If possession is ordered on this Ground, the landlord will have to pay the tenant's removal expenses.

5. Suitable Alternative Accommodation

If there is somewhere else available for the tenant to live, this may be a reason for making a possession order under Ground 9. Usually the alternative accommodation will be somewhere offered by the present landlord but it does not need to be. Accommodation provided by the local authority or even owned by the tenant himself could be sufficient. In considering this Ground the court first has to decide if the alternative accommodation actually is *suitable*. Relevant to this is are matters such as the size of the property, the rent, how convenient it is for the tenant's work and the sort of furniture that will be provided. If the court does consider it suitable, it will usually exercise its discretion to make an order in favour of the landlord. However in some cases it might feel so sorry for the tenant as to take the opposite course. An elderly person who was distressed at having to move from a longstanding home would be the obvious example (although in respect of tenancies granted after 14 January 1989 there is obviously a limit to the amount of force this argument could have). A person who has become strongly immersed in the social life of an area or a block of flats might be able to persuade a court not to make a possession order forcing him to live somewhere else. Considerations such as these would of course have to be balanced against any hardship that would be caused to the landlord by declining to grant the possession order.

As with the redevelopment Ground, if a court does make a possession order on this basis it will order the landlord to pay the tenant's removal expenses.

6. Termination of Employment

Where the property was let as a consequence of the tenant's employment and that employment ends, possession may be ordered pursuant to Ground 16. If the tenant had been allowed to live in the property because doing so was essential for him to perform his duties, there will not be a tenancy at all (see page 22) and the landlord's task will be that much simpler. However if the landlord owns property near, say, a factory that he lets out to his employees in the hope of making it easier for them to get to work on time, there will be a tenancy. In that instance this Ground could apply. In exercising its discretion the court is likely to take into account the reason the employee left. One who was dismissed without a good reason will generally be treated more sympathetically than one who has resigned or been sacked for misconduct.

7. Death of the tenant

Where the tenancy was granted after 14 January 1989 and the tenant dies, the tenancy comes to an end. However the tenancy may pass under his will or his intestacy. If the person to whom it passes is not living in the premises the landlord would automatically be entitled to possession because it would not then be a residential tenancy. In practice tenants rarely think of tenancies as assets which can be left in wills. If tenant makes a will which makes no specific reference to the tenancy it will pass to the person who has been left the *residue* of the estate. Intestacy is the most likely means by which the tenancy may pass. If the person to whom the tenancy passes is living in the premises he will become the tenant.

In some circumstances the person who becomes a tenant will have the right to succeed to the tenancy (see pages 63 to 65). If those circumstances do not apply, the landlord will have an automatic right to possession under the mandatory Ground 7. To be able to rely on this the landlord must commence proceedings within a year of the tenant's death or, if later, within a year of finding out about that death. The landlord may accept rent during that time without losing his rights under Ground 7. However if he agrees in writing to a change in the terms of the tenancy, perhaps increasing the rent, during that period a new assured tenancy, to which Ground 7 will not apply, will be created.

Giving notice to end tenancies granted after 14 January 1989

Before the landlord can obtain possession of a property he has to serve a notice on the tenant warning him of his intention to seek possession. There is nothing to prevent him merely asking the tenant to go informally by a letter or even just speaking to him. However if the tenant stays, the landlord will have to obtain a court order and it will be necessary to have served the notice to do this.

This notice has to be in the official form, which is set out on page 108. Immediately following it are the more common Grounds that should be inserted onto the notice if they apply. If there is more than one tenant, it must be addressed to both or all of them. For some Grounds the landlord needs to give at least two months' notice. These are where:

- the landlord has previously lived or intends living in the premises (Ground 1);
- a mortgagee seeks possession on the basis of a Ground 1 notice (Ground 2);
- the property is required for a minister of religion, the appropriate notice having been given before the tenancy commenced (Ground 5);
- a new tenancy was created on the death of the previous tenant (Ground 6);
- the landlord wants to redevelop the property (Ground 7);
- the landlord is relying on suitable alternative accommodation being available (Ground 9); or
- where the property was let in consequence of the tenant's employment (Ground 16).

In other cases the landlord needs only give two weeks' notice. However if the tenancy is one where the tenant pays rent every month, the landlord will have to give a month's notice running from the date when rent is next due. If rent is paid quarterly, he will have to give a quarter's notice whatever Grounds are relied upon. The landlord may rely upon more than one Ground, but will have to give the longer period of notice if any of the Grounds which require it are specified. The landlord must specify which Grounds he is relying upon and set out what each ground is.

Once the notice is served, the landlord has twelve months to commence proceedings. The court is more likely to exercise its discretion in favour of the landlord if he has commenced proceedings shortly after serving the notice, particularly if claim is based on Grounds relating to the tenant's misconduct.

If the landlord fails to serve the notice, the court may still make a possession order. Once again the court has to considers whether it is *just and equitable* to dispense with the notice. If the landlord has told the tenant that he was seeking possession, but not served any notice it is more likely that the court would be willing to dispense with the notice. If the tenant has had no warning at all of the landlord's intention, then it is highly unlikely that the notice would be dispensed with. If on the other hand the notice was served but contained a minor defect, it would probably be treated as valid under this provision. There is no power to dispense with the notice in a claim based on Ground 8 (three months' arrears of rent). However even if that Ground cannot be relied upon in the absence of a proper notice, the court could usually still make a possession order on the other rent Grounds (10 and 11).

Possession under assured shorthold tenancies

The landlord has an automatic right to possession at the end of the term of an assured shorthold tenancy and does not need to show that any of the statutory Grounds apply. The procedure for granting such tenancies was discussed on pages 20. The landlord must give at least two month's notice to the tenant, or if appropriate both or all of the tenants, that he requires possession. The notice may be given before the fixed term has finished but must not expire until after then.

Notice can be given at any time after the expiry of the fixed term if the tenant carries on living at the premises, but it still needs to give the tenant at least two months' warning. Notice which expires after the term of the tenancy has ended must expire on a date when the tenant is due to pay rent.

The notice need not be in any particular form: an example of words that could be used is contained on page 108. The rather convoluted way this is set out has the effect that so long as the landlord specifies a two month period, the notice will automatically expire on a permitted date.

Grounds for possession under tenancies granted before 15 January 1989

Instead of there being *Grounds* for possession where the tenancy was granted before 15 January 1989, there are *Cases*, which are listed in Schedule 15 to the Rent Act 1977 and two other basis that are listed in other parts of that Act. Although there are twenty-one situations where possession can be granted, these apply in a considerably narrower range of circumstance than did the sixteen under the Housing Act 1988. Cases 1 to 10 are discretionary, Cases 11 to 20 are mandatory (Case 7 has been repealed), one of the others is discretionary and one mandatory. The court has similar powers to suspend possession orders as it does for later tenancies (see page 74).

1. Nonpayment of rent

Where there are any rent arrears the court has a discretion to make an order for possession (Case 1). This Case also covers any other breaches of the tenancy agreement by the tenant, such as keeping a pet when one is prohibited.

2. Other misbehaviour by the tenant

Cases 2, 3 and 4 cover very similar situations to those described under the same heading in respect of tenancies subject to the Housing Act 1988 and Grounds 14, 13 and 15 respectively (see pages 75 to 76). There are other Cases which loosely fit under this heading. These are:

- The tenant has given notice to quit and then changes his mind but the landlord has already taken steps to relet or sell the property (Case 5);
- the tenant sublets the whole of the property without the landlord's consent (Case 6); and
- the tenant sublets part of the property at a higher rent than he is paying himself in respect of that part (Case 10).

3. Where the landlord has served a notice before the tenancy commenced

The most frequent situation where the landlord could serve a notice was when he had lived in the property himself previously *and* subsequently required it as a residence for himself or a member of his family (Case 11). A mortgagee who has taken over the landlord's interest can claim possession under this Case, as can the person to whom the property passed on the landlord's death. The landlord can also rely on this Case, if he wants to sell the property so that he use the proceeds to buy a home nearer to where he works.

If a landlord bought a home he intended to live in after retiring from work, he could serve a notice under Case 12. On retirement he would then be able to recover possession in similar circumstances to those which applied under Case 11. Case 12 though did not extend to the situation where he required for the property as a residence for his family members rather than himself.

Case 20 provided for members of the regular armed forces to be able to let property without necessarily having lived there first and recover them in similar circumstances to Case 11. This Case also did not extend to situations where recovery was sought because the landlord wanted to provide a residence for members of his family rather than himself.

Cases 13 to 18 enabled notices to be served in less common situations such as out of season holiday lettings and lettings of property usually used by ministers of religion.

Case 19 applies where there was a *protected shorthold tenancy*. In many ways this was similar to a shorthold assured tenancy. Advance notice had to be served on the tenant, informing him the property was to be let as an assured shorthold. the tenancy had to be for a term between one and five years. If the tenant continued in occupation after the expiry of the term the landlord retains his rights to obtain possession.

In respect of Cases 11, 12, 19 and 20, if notice was not served before the commencement of the tenancy, the landlord might be able persuade the court to order possession nonetheless. The court's discretion to do this would be exercised on the same principles as it would be in considering an application under Housing Act 1988 Ground 1 discussed on pages to 77. Significantly there was a discretion to dispense with the initial notice requirement in relation to a protected shorthold tenancy although there is no such power in relation to an assured shorthold tenancy.

4. Termination of employment

Case 8, provides the landlord with a potential right to possession in similar circumstances to Ground 16 discussed under the same heading in relation to the Housing Act 1988 (see pages 78). However for Case 8 to apply the landlord must also now require the property to let to another employee in addition to the fact that it was let to the present tenant in consequence of his employment.

5. Landlord's requirements for the property

If the landlord wants the property as a home for himself his parents or his children, then that may be sufficient to justify a possession order (Case 9). This Case will not normally be available to a landlord who bought his interest in the property after the tenancy was granted by the previous owner.

6. Suitable Alternative Accommodation

Section 98 of the Rent Act 1977 contains a discretionary ground for ordering possession that applies in very similar circumstances to those applicable when the landlord makes such a claim under the Housing Act 1988, which is discussed under the same heading on pages 77 to 78. The requirement to pay the tenant's removal costs does not however apply.

7. Overcrowding

Where the property becomes overcrowded within the statutory definition the landlord has a mandatory right to possession (s101 Rent Act 1977). This definition is exceedingly complex and outside the scope of this book. It is likely to apply if people of the opposite sex over the age of ten other than couples have to share a room.

Giving notice to end tenancies granted before 15 January 1989

In some circumstances a *notice to quit* is required to terminate a tenancy granted before 15 January 1989. If the tenancy has never been for a fixed term, then the notice will be necessary. This will be the case where it was originally agreed that the tenant would pay rent on a weekly or monthly basis indefinitely and he has carried on doing so. If the tenancy has been for a fixed term, say one year, and has expired with the tenant remaining in occupation, the notice will not be necessary but it may be advisable to serve one anyway. A notice to quit must contain specified information. A blank form of notice appears on page 109. It must, if rent is paid weekly, give at least 28 days' notice effective from when the next instalment of rent is due. If the rent is paid monthly or quarterly, then those periods are the minimum periods of notice. Yearly tenancies however require only six months' notice. If there is more than one tenant, the notice must be addressed to all or both of them.

To give an example, suppose a tenant pays rent every Monday. On Wednesday 3rd July 1995 the landlord decides to serve a notice to quit. He can serve the notice immediately but it must give 28 days notice from Monday 8th July, the date when the next rent is due. That notice should therefore expire on Monday 5th August. If the tenant paid rent monthly on the first of the month, then notice given on 3rd July should expire on 1 September, one month after the date when the next payment of rent is due.

If a notice to quit is not served when needed, the court has no discretion to order possession. As the landlord had no right to possession at the time he started the action, his claim cannot succeed and will be thrown out.

Evicting the tenant without a court order

However tempting it may be; however much a landlord may feel he has been abused by a tenant; however frustrated he is by delays in the legal system, he should not even think about evicting a tenant without a court order. If he does, he will incur the ire of the civil and often the criminal law. The type of tenant who has reduced the landlord to this level of anger will inevitably relish being able to use the legal system exact revenge upon him.

The Protection from Eviction Act 1977 makes virtually any form of harassment of a tenant by a landlord or his agent serious offences. This can apply to acts far short of actually evicting the tenant. Persistently withholding services such as electricity or water can be sufficient, violence, threats of violence and persistent oral abuse are other examples of harassment.

If the landlord does find himself being prosecuted for such behaviour, the matter can be tried either by magistrates: usually the accused landlord will at least get the dubious honour of choosing which. On conviction by magistrates the landlord may get six months' imprisonment and a fine of up to £5,000, in the Crown Court that can be two years and an unlimited fine. Of course, it is only in the most extreme cases that the maximum penalties or any form of imprisonment would be imposed.

An illegally evicted tenant will also have a civil claim for damages. He will be entitled to compensation for any financial loss suffered. If, for instance, after being evicted he had to stay in a hotel until he could find another place to rent, the landlord will be ordered to reimburse his bills. If his possessions are damaged or lost in the course of the eviction the landlord will have to replace them. On top of this there will be damages to compensate him for the sheer unpleasantness of losing his home. If he has been assaulted or threatened in the process of the eviction, these damages will rocket.

Finally, in an effort to ensure the landlord does not gain from his illegal action the law will require the landlord to pay to the tenant the difference between the market value of the premises when they were subject to the tenancy and when they were not. Where there is a tenant who had the benefit of the protection of the Rent Act 1977 because the tenancy was granted before 15 January 1989, this can amount to getting on for half the value of the premises. If the tenant gets back into possession whether or not as a result of a court order, the landlord will not have to pay this head of damages.

Even once the landlord has obtained a possession order, an attempt to evict the tenant except pursuant to a warrant, which is issued separately by the court and executed by certified bailiffs (see pages 97 to 98), is still illegal for these purposes.

The law is less draconian if the landlord and the tenant share accommodation at the premises and the premises constitute the landlord's only or main home. However even in those circumstances evicting someone without a court order would be asking for trouble. Regardless of the niceties of landlord and tenant law, the landlord would lay himself open to allegations of assault and stealing the tenant's possessions.

If either a landlord or a tenant believes that a wrongful eviction claim may have arisen they would be well advised to see a solicitor.

From the Tenant's Perspective

Actions by mortgagees

If the landlord served a Ground 1 notice in respect of a tenancy granted after 14 January 1989, a mortgagee who takes possession of the property will also be able to rely on the notice. A mortgagee is most likely to be able to do this where a landlord has fallen into arrears with his payments. Even if the landlord has failed to serve the notice but could have served it, the court may order possession in these circumstances. In practice, it is less likely to do so than where the landlord himself is seeking possession having forgotten to serve the notice. If the landlord granted the tenancy without seeking the consent of his mortgagee and did so in breach of his mortgage agreement, the tenant may not even be entitled to remain in possession until the end of the contractual term.

Mortgagees who have taken possession of premises are sometimes willing for tenants to remain in occupation so long of course as the tenants are willing to continue paying rent to the mortgagees. Evicting tenants who have behaved entirely properly has sometimes brought bad publicity upon banks and building societies. To avoid this, such organisations are often willing to allow a reasonably long period for the tenant to remain in the property. Used subtly the threat of publicity may be fairly productive. Banks and building societies often possess incredibly inefficient legal departments and may, even if not prepared to negotiate with the tenants, take months to commence possession proceedings.

When the landlord sells his interest in the property the purchaser will not be able to rely on the Ground 1 notice.

The fact that a mortgagee requires possession was one of the circumstances in which possession could be obtained under a tenancy granted before 15 January 1989. This was dependent upon there having been a Case 11 notice or the court believing it would be fair to dispense with such a notice (see page 81).

When the tenant wishes to terminate the agreement

A tenancy for a fixed term obliges the tenant to pay rent throughout the period of the term. Just as the landlord is not be entitled to evict a tenant until the term has run out, the tenant is not able to leave. In practice it may well be that most landlords would not bother taking any action if a tenant did walk out, but that of course does not alter the tenant's legal and moral obligations. Many tenancy agreements have the effect of preventing the tenant escaping his obligations even by finding a replacement. However in practice if the tenant does find a reasonably respectable person willing to take his place, it would be ridiculous for the landlord to refuse it. Should the landlord attempt to recover the rent for the remainder of the period from the tenant, his claim may well be disallowed because he has then failed to *mitigate* his loss. In this situation it is the tenant rather than the landlord who should go to the trouble and expense of finding the replacement tenant. Should another tenant be found but subsequently fail to pay rent, the landlord will still be entitled to look to the original tenant for reimbursement during the remainder of the term.

In the case of a tenancy that is not for a fixed period the tenant must give at least four weeks' notice to bring it to an end. This notice must expire on a day when rent is otherwise due to paid. The notice given by the tenant has to be in writing but need not follow any particular form. A simple letter is the best way to do it.

An example of such a letter sent in February 1995 might be:
Dear Landlord,
I am writing to let you know I shall be leaving the property on 31 March 1995. Perhaps you could please contact me to discuss the necessary arrangements and to return my deposit.
Yours sincerely,

10. GOING TO COURT

From the Landlord's Perspective

The county court

Claims for possession of residential premises should almost invariably be brought in the county court. The procedure for starting a possession action varies depending on the basis on which possession is claimed. There are four different procedures which will be discussed separately. Whichever procedure is used, the landlord must first decide which county court he is going to start the case in. There are around 300 different such courts in England & Wales. Each has a specific geographical area. They are listed in phone books (under Courts!).

Proceedings should be started in the court which covers the area where the property is situated. It isn't always easy to find out which court, particularly in London, covers which area. If an action is commenced in the wrong court, that court should either accept jurisdiction or transfer the proceedings to the correct court. The latter task can take several weeks. A telephone enquiry beforehand should establish whether the court one envisages issuing the proceedings in is the correct court for that location. There are many county courts where the staff take pride in being as awkward as possible, and for them finding fault with the form of a claim so as to be able to return it represents a major triumph. There is probably not much one can to do to avoid this other than triple checking the paperwork as carefully as possible. It will often be necessary to visit the county court to obtain the correct form to commence the action on. If the form can be completed there and then, asking a member of the court staff to check it may decrease the chances of an arbitrary rejection, but this can never be guaranteed.

The person bringing the claim is the *plaintiff* and it is brought against the *defendant*.

A fee has to be paid on commencement of proceedings. If the claim is for possession alone, that fee is at the time of writing £50. If arrears of rent or damages, perhaps for damage caused to the property, are claimed, then the fee will be 10% of the amount claimed if that does not exceed £500. Between

£500 and £1,000 it is £60. Between £1,000 and £5,000, £70; over £5,000, £80. These are subject to the £50 minimum if there is a possession claim. Otherwise the minimum fee is £10. They frequently change (upwards!) and should be checked when starting an action. Other fees are charged at various stages of the case.

Rent cases

The form by which landlords start actions for possession orders where there are arrears of rent was simplified in November 1993. This appears to have been done with the aim of reducing legal costs and making it easier for landlords who wished to proceed without a solicitor at all. Ironically in some cases costs have been increased by solicitors unaware of these new procedures starting actions in the more complex old forms and then having to use the new form as well.

There is now a printed county court form on which the landlord submits details of his case (form N119). This contains a request for information that it would not have been appropriate to include in the old style particulars of claim, for instance about the defendant's financial position. As well as this form the landlord should complete the standard form of possession summons (N5).

Possession pursuant to a notice served before the tenancy was granted

Where the landlord has served a notice before the tenancy was granted saying that it was an assured shorthold tenancy (see pages 20) or that Ground 1 applied (see pages 20 to 21), then the procedure for obtaining possession can be much simpler and shorter without the need for any hearing at all. This, like the procedure in rent arrears cases, has been introduced recently. A mortgagee claiming possession under Ground 2 cannot use this procedure. The landlord starts the action on a standard form available from the county court (form N5A). This form once completed is an affidavit, which means the landlord has to swear it. Swearing an affidavit can be done in the court office or in front of most solicitors who will charge a nominal fee.

The form contains well drafted explanatory notes, which specify which of the many alternatives it provides should be deleted in any particular situation. Filling it in should not present any problems but as with any form that asks a lot of questions and involves a degree of cross-referencing it is easy to become confused. The importance of setting aside time to do the form properly cannot be stressed enough. It will be necessary to provide copies of the notices and *exhibit* them to the affidavit. This means the person in front of whom the affidavit is sworn verifies the fact that these copies are attached.

Once the form is submitted and sent on by the court to the tenant he has fourteen days to reply. If no reply is received, the landlord can then request the court to make a possession order. If the tenant replies, raising something that the judge who considers the papers believes means he could have a defence to the claim, a hearing will be ordered. If the tenant's reply does not raise anything of substance, a possession order will be made without any hearing.

Landlords cannot use this procedure if they are also claiming rent arrears. If there are arrears of rent, they can still use this procedure to obtain possession then start a fresh action for rent arrears. Alternatively they can start an action under the general procedure claiming both possession and arrears of rent. Rarely in practice will a landlord actually obtain rent arrears from a tenant after he has been evicted from the premises.

There is a similar procedure for pre-15 January 1989 tenancies where notices were served which entitle the landlord to possession were served before the tenancy commenced. If this procedure is used, the hearing can be at any time after fourteen days, in some cases seven days. The application has to be made on a specified form: which form depends upon the basis on which the notice was served, and must be accompanied by an affidavit which sets out the basis on which the landlord is claiming possession and exhibits the relevant documents. As with the procedure for later tenancies, rent cannot be recovered, though can be the subject of a separate action.

Squatters

Where the occupants of the property are not and have never been tenants, the owner may use a procedure that is designed to enable him to obtain a possession order very quickly. This procedure is designed primarily to remove squatters. It would not be appropriate in a case where someone has been granted a "licence" because the property owner hoped to avoid giving statutory protection to the tenants. As a device for getting rid of lodgers it will often succeed, but if the lodger has been in the property for a long time, the court may insist on the landlord using the general procedure discussed in the next section.

In cases of tremendous urgency it is sometimes better to commence the action using this procedure in the High Court where a hearing date may be available more quickly. A property owner contemplating such a course will however need the help of a solicitor.

The application is commenced on the county court form N312 . This form is sent to the court along with an affidavit which must state the following:

- whether the Plaintiff owns the land as freeholder, leaseholder or has some other interest;
- the circumstances in which it is being occupied without his permission; and
- that he does not know the name of any person occupying the land other than those he has named as the Defendants.

In the case of squatters, whose names the landlord does not know, the defendants can be referred to as "persons unknown". This application has to be served in a way that will draw it to the occupier's attention. Usually the court will arrange that. If it cannot do so or is likely to cause a long delay, it will be necessary for the property owner to instruct a solicitor.

A hearing should be arranged by the court within a week or so of the papers being sent to the tenants. At this hearing the judge will read the Plaintiff's papers and give the Defendant a chance to say what he wants by way of reply. If it turns out that there are arguments why the occupier might be entitled to remain in possession, a full hearing will be ordered. If there clearly is no defence the court will order possession usually with immediate effect. Such an order will not however be enforced immediately (see pages 97 to 98).

Other cases, the general procedure

Where possession is not claimed on the basis of rent arrears or a notice of the sort discussed above, the action is started by the landlord using the general county court form (N4) applicable to what are known as *fixed date actions*. As well as straightforward details this needs to contain a statement of why the landlord believes he is entitled to possession, known as the *particulars of claim*. Drafting this is quite a skilled job and many landlords do seek the help of a solicitor to do it. The particulars must give the following information:

- The fact that the plaintiff is the landlord and the defendant the tenant;
- When the tenancy commenced;
- Which of the statutory Grounds or Cases for possession apply (if the landlord claims there is not in fact a tenancy he should say so instead of citing this reasons);
- The details of what has happened to make those Grounds or Cases apply;
- The date when any notice seeking possession or notice to quit was served and when it took effect;
- Details of any damages the landlord is claiming;
- The fact that the landlord seeks possession and (if appropriate) damages;
- If a large amount of money is owing, the landlord should also request interest "pursuant to s69 County Courts Act 1984"; and
- For the period after the notice terminating the tenancy has come to an end, *mesne profits* should be sought. This is because then the landlord is claiming there is no longer a tenancy and that *rent* payments would no longer be appropriate.

There is no need to dress this information up in legalese. Laypeople's attempts to make documents read as if they were drafted by lawyers almost always result in an embarrassingly ungrammatical and pompous mess. Using ordinary language, the simpler the better, is to be preferred.

Adding some hypothetical facts to the tenancy of 41a Wilson Road, and assuming it had been let to John Skinner, Jack Heffer and James Rooker: at the end of the yearly term these tenants carried on in occupation of the property. They have had a succession of late night parties and the neighbours have complained to Mrs Healey. She serves the appropriate notice and commences possession proceedings.

These are the Particulars of Claim she might use to commence an action at the end of May 1996.

IN THE BOW COUNTY COURT
Between
Angela H Healey   Plaintiff
and
(1) John Skinner
(2) Jack Heffer
(3) James Rooker   Defendants

PARTICULARS OF CLAIM

1. The Plaintiff is the owner of the freehold of the property known as 41a Wilson Road, Stratford, London E15 ("the property").

2. By a tenancy agreement dated 31 January 1995 the Plaintiff granted to the Defendants a tenancy of the property for a term of one year from 1 February 1995 ("the tenancy").

3. Under the tenancy the Defendants pay a rent to the Plaintiff of £180 per week.

3. The tenancy was subject to the provisions of the Housing Act 1988.

4. The tenants have remained in possession of the property as statutory tenants under the provisions of the said Housing Act 1988.

5. On 1 May 1996 the Plaintiff served on the Defendants a notice pursuant to section 8 of the said Housing Act 1988 stating that possession would be sought pursuant to Grounds 12 and 13 of Schedule 2 to the said Housing Act 1988 not earlier than 17 May 1996.

6. The Plaintiff is entitled to possession on the basis of the said Grounds.

PARTICULARS

On 14 March 1996, 28 March 1996, 11 April 1996 and 25 April 1996 the Defendants have held noisy parties at the property which have lasted until at least 3 a.m. As a result of each of those parties occupants of adjoining properties have complained to the Plaintiff.

By covenant (x) of the said tenancy agreement, the Defendants covenanted not to permit or allow anything to be done on the premises which may be or become a nuisance or annoyance to the occupiers of any adjoining premises.

The Plaintiff therefore claims:
(i) Possession of the property;

93

(ii) Mesne profits at the rate of £180 per week until possession of the property be given to the Plaintiff.

These particulars of course are the sort that are likely to be drafted by lawyers acting on Mrs Healey's behalf. There is no need for landlords doing their own to aspire to this particular style, but it may nonetheless be useful to have a professional model as a starting point.

The hearing

Where proceedings are commenced using the general procedure or the "rent arrears" forms, the matter will be listed for a hearing. This will sometimes be before a *circuit judge* and sometimes a *district judge*. Circuit judges are one step higher up the judicial hierarchy than district judges. It makes little difference to the parties which their case is listed before, except that district judge's lists are usually better managed, meaning less time spent waiting around at court. If the tenant fails to put in any defence disputing the claim and doesn't attend the hearing, the landlord is unlikely to have any difficulty obtaining a possession order. It will still be necessary for him to turn up at court with all the relevant documents and any witnesses who can explain matters that the landlord does not have first hand knowledge of.

In many county courts the first hearing will be listed at the same time as a number of other cases. The expectation is that none of these cases will take longer than a few minutes. If the tenant comes to court and raises matters that the judge feels could give him a defence, the hearing will be adjourned for a *trial* on a date when the court can set aside more time for it. Sometimes the court will not set such a date there and then. It may direct that the defendant first serve a formal *defence* setting out what his case is. After that the parties will have to send each other lists and copies of any relevant documents (known as *discovery* and *inspection*) followed by written statements of what their evidence is. These statements should be more detailed than the particulars of claim and defence. These procedures can take weeks, even months. It is particularly frustrating for a landlord to have his possession claim delayed while this is done. Some judges will go out of their way to speed matters up. It may be worthwhile asking the judge to make an order that the defendant pay the rent until the hearing. The judge will normally only agree to such an order if he thinks it realistic to expect the defendant to pay the money. If the tenant has persuaded the judge that he does have an arguable defence to the claim, it would be advisable for the landlord to consult a solicitor. There may well be a technical defence, such as a defect in a notice, to which there is no answer. If the landlord pursues a fatally flawed case through all the procedural steps to a trial he may end paying a substantial amount towards the tenant's legal costs. It is much better to have a professional appraisal of the case at an early stage.

At the trial the landlord bringing the claim will have to start his case by explaining to the judge what it is about and referring him to all the relevant documents. The landlord will then give evidence himself and have the opportunity to call any witnesses he wants. After that the tenant will give evidence. The landlord will have the opportunity to ask him questions- *cross-examine* him. After that the parties, starting (somewhat illogically) with the tenant, can each make a further speech to the judge. If a party is represented by a lawyer, that lawyer will do all the speech making and questioning for him.

The judge will then make a decision, in complicated cases giving reasons why he did so. He may decide to make a possession order but suspend it on conditions, most commonly that the tenant pay off the arrears of rent and future rent (the suspending of possession orders is discussed on page 74). Either party can appeal against the judge's decision. However the rights of appeal are largely restricted to points of law and such a course should not be taken without legal advice.

Costs

When a person wins a case, the court will normally make a *costs order* in that person's favour. This is directed primarily towards the costs of employing lawyers to fight the case. Where someone has won a case without a lawyer he can claim £8 per hour for their time in preparing the case. Whether or not a lawyer has been used, the landlord can claim out of pocket expenses for himself and witnesses and of course the court fee. If the costs are relatively small, as they should be if the order is made at the first hearing, the judge will usually assess a figure when making the possession order. If they are substantial the judge will order them to be subject to more detailed assessment, a process known as *taxing*. This is likely to result in the other side being ordered to pay considerably less than the litigant has to pay his own solicitor. The solicitor is entitled to his agreed fee regardless of the amount assessed. If no fee was agreed with the solicitor, the litigant is entitled to insist on solicitor's bill being assessed. The solicitor should provide details of how this can be done when he submits his bill. Assessment in this situation is done on a different basis to one that decides how much the other party has to pay, and the landlord is still likely to be out of pocket.

> **To give an example, suppose a landlord has obtained a possession order on the basis of the tenants having committed various acts of nuisance at the property. They contested the case and it went to a full trial which lasted a whole day. The solicitors' bill for that and all the preliminary work might well be £1,500. The court might make an order that the tenants pay those costs. However the tenants would have the right to have those costs assessed or taxed. Such an assessment might result in them only being required to pay £1,000, towards the £1,500 the landlord would have to pay his own solicitors. If the landlord thought his solicitors' bill was too, much he could apply to have it assessed. It is unlikely that it would be reduced to anything like as low a figure as the tenants would have to pay. It might well be assessed on this basis as £1,450 if reduced at all..**

In practice the chances are that a tenant against whom a costs order is made is unlikely to pay them, just as he is unlikely to pay any arrears of rent or damages. If there is a surety, it should be possible to recover the costs against that person although ultimately it may be necessary to bring a separate court action to do so. If the other party is granted legal aid, the court will usually make a costs order, but prohibit the winner from attempting to enforce it unless he obtains the court's permission to do so. This permission would only be granted where the other person's financial position has improved considerably since he was granted legal aid. It might be worthwhile applying for permission a few years later if the tenant had been a student at the time of the court order, subsequently gets his qualification and obtains a good job. The landlord can make the application in the six years following the making of the order. In practice this is rarely done, if only because after litigation the parties do not usually keep in touch with other and the landlord will not know what has happened to the tenant.

Legal aid

There are two criteria for being eligible for *legal aid*: the merits of the case and one's financial position. Most solicitors will provide an initial consultation without charging, during which they will advise whether it is worth making a legal aid application. The solicitor will be able to give a preliminary view on whether the case is meritorious enough for legal aid to be appropriate. Financial eligibility is related to income and savings. An income and savings above certain limits mean the person will not be eligible at all. A lower income or savings will mean a contribution will have to be paid towards the legal aid. The relevant levels are frequently altered. From the income figure expenditure which relate to matters such as housing and travel to work can be disregarded.

In some circumstances where legal aid is granted and property is recovered, the Legal Aid Board, which adminsters the scheme, will have a right to so much of that property as is needed to repay the fees the Board has paid to the solicitor. The solicitor will explain this in detail when the legal aid application is made.

If a person has legal aid and loses the case, the normal rule that the loser pays the winner's costs is not usually applied. In some circumstances this of itself can prove an even better reason for being legally aided than the advantages of having representation by a solicitor.

Enforcement

Once a court has made an order for possession there is no guarantee that the tenant will leave immediately or even by the latest date the judge had allowed him to remain until. Once that last date has expired if the tenant remains in possession, the landlord has to obtain a *warrant of possession* from the court office. (It is not possible to obtain this in advance of that date in anticipation of the tenants not leaving when they ought to.) To obtain this warrant it is necessary to fill in another form (N325, unless it was a "squatters' action, when it is form N52) and pay a further fee of £50. The bailiff will normally then set a date in a few weeks time when the tenant will be evicted. He will visit the tenant first to give him warning of the application.

Once the tenant has been evicted the landlord would be well advised to immediately change the locks on the property and if necessary board it up.

There is surprisingly little sanction against a tenant who breaks back in after being evicted.

Applications by tenants who have hitherto completely ignored the proceedings are sometimes made a day or two before a warrant is due to be enforced. Such an application can in certain circumstances even be made without the landlord having any opportunity to present his case. These applications often succeed largely because of the desire of the courts to avoid the social problems caused by making people homeless if at all possible. The result will be a wait of several further weeks before the landlord can actually get possession, however feeble the tenant's case. To say such delays are immensely frustrating for the landlord is an understatement.

Judgements for the payment of money can be enforced in a number of different ways. The most effective is often an *attachment of earnings order*. The procedure in respect of such enforcement is though outside the scope of this book.

From the Tenant's Perspective

Claims by tenants

Disrepair and harassment are the two main basis for tenants making claims against their landlords. (See pages 42 and 84 respectively for discussions of when the circumstances enabling such claims to be made arise). If a landlord has physically evicted a tenant from a property, then it is likely that tenant will be able to obtain an order for very substantial damages. The tenant may be able to obtain an order known as an *injunction* requiring the landlord to let him back into the premises. Similarly in disrepair cases it may be possible to obtain an injunction requiring the landlord to carry out repairs. Obtaining these remedies is extremely complex and is not practical without the help of a solicitor.

Claiming damages is considerably more intricate than claiming rent arrears. It is often difficult to establish whether the tenant is entitled to anything at all. If he is entitled, assessing damages is much more difficult than merely stating that rent arrears at say £50 per week over ten weeks have built up. For this reason it is probably a good idea for tenants bring such claims to seek the advice of a solicitor before doing so.

However where the claim is only for a small amount, perhaps the landlord's initial failure to repair the roof has resulted in water leaking onto and spoiling a rug owned by the tenant, it might be worth bringing a claim without incurring the expense of a solicitor. Legal aid is unlikely to be available if the value of the claim is less than around £1,500. If the amount claimed is under £1,000, the case will automatically be referred to *arbitration* which is a relatively informal private hearing.

Claims for damages can be commenced using, if the tenant can quantify the amount claimed precisely, form N1, if not form N2. An order for costs, other than the court fee, will not be made when a claim has been referred to arbitration because of the small amount of money involved.

When a landlord makes a possession claim, the tenant may be entitled to make a claim of his own against the landlord, a *counterclaim*. The forms the court will send him notifying him of the landlords claim will, unless the landlord uses the special procedure, ask if he wishes to make a counterclaim. If the tenant decides to deal with this without instructing a solicitor, he should set out in as straight-forward language as possible the basis for this. He will then eventually get the same opportunity to present his claim as the landlord.

Claims by landlords

A tenant faced with a possession claim made by a landlord but who wants to stay in position should seek the advice of a solicitor about whether or not there is any potential defence. Often an experienced eye will pick up technicalities that can defeat or at least substantially delay the landlord's claim. Many solicitors make no charge for an initial interview. Legal aid is discussed at page 97. In practice tenants, generally being poorer than landlords, are far more likely to be eligible for legal aid.

If the claim is based upon rent arrears it is important for the tenant to attend court. There may not be any real defence, but particularly if there are less than three months' arrears, the court may be persuaded not to make a possession order if the rent and something towards the arrears is paid regularly in future (suspended possession orders are discussed on pages 74 to 74).

Last minute applications by tenants to stave off the enforcement of possession are discussed on page 98. Whilst such applications can succeed, to rely on one doing so is most unwise. Many judges will be most unsympathetic to anyone who has been unnecessarily slow in responding to the proceedings. Tenants, like anyone else faced with a legal claim, should do all they can to protect their position at the earliest possible moment. Likewise once an order for possession has been made, it is advisable to start looking for somewhere else to live. Leaving it to the last possible moment is virtually asking to be made homeless.

Sometimes the local authority will be obliged to rehouse a person who has been the subject of a possession order. A tenant who feels this might be a possibility in his case should consult the housing department of the relevant authority as soon as is possible.

11. FORMS

Notice of an assured shorthold tenancy

Housing Act 1988 section 20

●Please write clearly in black ink

●If there is anything you do not understand you should get advice from a solicitor or a Citizens' Advice bureau, before you agree to the tenancy

●The landlord must give this notice to the tenant before an assured shorthold tenancy is granted. it does not commit the tenant to take the tenancy.

●**This document is important, keep it in a safe place.**

To..
.... *name of proposed tenant, if a joint tenancy is being offered enter the names of the joint tenants*

1. You are proposing to take a tenancy of the dwelling house known as:
....
....
....

from   /   /19   to   /   /19   *The tenancy must*
be for a

term certain of at least six months

2. This notice is to tell you that your tenancy is to be an assured shorthold tenancy. Provided you keep to the terms of the tenancy, you are entitled to remain in the dwelling for at least the first six months of the fixed period agreed at the start of the tenancy. At the end of this period, depending on the terms of the tenancy, the landlord may have the right to repossession if he wants.

3. The rent for this tenancy is the rent we have agreed. However, you have the right to apply to a rent assessment committee for a determination of the rent which the committee considers might reasonably have been obtained under the tenancy. If the committee considers (i) that there is a sufficient number of similar properties int he locality let on assured tenancies and that (ii) the rent we have agreed is significantly higher than the rent which might   reasonably be obtained having regard to the level of the rents for other assured tenancies in the locality, it will determine a rent for the tenancy. That rent will be the legal maximum you can be required to pay from the date the committee directs.

If the rent incudes council tax, the rent determined by the committee will be inclusive of council tax.

To be signed by the landlord or his agent (someone acting for him). If there are joint landlords each must sign, unless one signs on behalf of the rest with their agreement.

Signed.................................

Name(s) of landlord(s)...

Address of landlord(s)...

Tel:...

If signed by agent, name and address of agent

Name of agent...

Address of agent...

Tel:...

Date   /   /19

Special note for existing tenants

●Generally if you already have a protected or statutory tenancy and you give it up to take a new tenancy in the same or other accommodation owned by the same landlord, that tenancy cannot be an assured tenancy. It can still be a protected tenancy.

●But if you currently occupy a dwelling which was let to you as a protected shorthold tenant, special rules apply.

●If you have an assured tenancy which is not a shorthold under the Housing Act 1988, you cannot be offered an assured shorthold tenancy of the same or other accommodation by the same landlord.

Tenancy agreement

This agreement is made [*date*] between [*landlord's name*] (hereinafter called "the landlord") and [*tenant's name*] (hereinafter called "the tenant").

It is agreed as follows:
The landlord will let and the tenants take the premises known as [*address of premises*] together with the fixtures, fittings, furniture and effects therein, which are listed in the attached inventory for a term of [*length*] (hereinafter called "the term") commencing on [*date*] at a rent of [*amount*] per [week *or* month] to be paid in advance on [*rent day or date*].

The tenant will:
(i) Pay the rent on the days and in the manner aforesaid, making the first payment on [*date*];

(ii) Pay to the landlord a deposit of [*amount*] as security for any loss including legal costs, which may for this purpose be assessed on an indemnity basis, which the landlord may suffer by reason of the tenant's failure to pay rent and observe the other covenants herein;

(iii) Pay for all gas and electricity consumed or supplied on or to the premises (including all fixed and standing charges) and all charges for maintenance and use of a telephone on the premises during the term;

(iv) Keep the interior of the premises clean and tidy and in as good a state of repair and decorative condition as at the beginning of the term, reasonable wear and tear excepted;

(v) Keep the contents clean;

(vi) Not remove any of the contents from the premises;

(vii) Replace any of the contents which may be destroyed or damaged so as to be unusable other than through fair wear and tear with others of similar value and appearance;

(viii)[*If appropriate*] Keep the garden clean and tidy and prevent it from becoming overgrown;

(ix) Not exhibit any poster or notice so that it is visible from outside the premises;

(x) Not permit or allow anything to be done on the premises which may be or become a nuisance or annoyance to the landlord or the occupiers of any adjoining premises or which may render the landlord's insurance of the premises void or voidable or increase the rate of such premium;

(xi) Not use or allow the premises to be used for any illegal or immoral purpose;

(xii) Not make any noise or play any radio, television set, stereo or similar device at the premises between 11 p.m. and 8 a.m. so as to be audible outside the premises;

(xiii) Not allow more than [*number appropriate to type of property*] people to reside or stay overnight at the premises;

(xiv) Not keep any animal at the premises;

(xv) Not block or cause any blockage to the drains and pipe gutters and channels in or about the premises;

(xvi) Not assign, underlet or part with possession of the whole or any part of the premises;

(xvii) Permit the landlord and the landlord's agents at reasonable times in daylight by appointment to enter the premises during the last 28 days of the term with prospective tenants and during any part of the term with prospective purchasers of the landlord's interest in the premises;

(xviii) Notify the landlord in writing of any defects in the premises as soon as practicable after the tenant has become aware of such defects; and

(xix) At the end of the term:

(a) Yield up the premises and the contents in such state of repair and condition as shall be in accordance with the tenant's obligations under this agreement;

(b) Make good or pay for the repair or replacement of such of the contents as have been broken, lost or damaged during the term;

(c) Pay for washing (including ironing and pressing) of all linen and for the washing and cleaning (including ironing and pressing) of all blankets, curtains and similar items which have been soiled during the tenancy; and

(d) Leave the contents in the rooms and places in which they were at the commencement of the term;

[*If there is more than one tenant*] And each tenant shall be responsible for the breach of any obligation hereunder by any other tenant as if he had broken the same himself, and shall be liable for the full rent regardless of any failure to contribute to the same by the other tenants or the fact that he or she or any or all of the others is no longer living at the premises.

The landlord will:

(i) Pay and indemnify the tenant against all rates assessments and outgoings and all water and sewerage charges in respect of the premises;

(ii) Keep the premises (though not the contents) insured against fire, flood, storm and similar risks;

(iii) Permit the tenant, so long as he or she pays the rent and performs his or her obligations under this agreement, quietly to use and enjoy the premises during the term without any interruption from the landlord or any person rightfully claiming under or in trust for the landlord;

(iv) Return to the tenant any rent payable for any period during which the premises may have been rendered uninhabitable by fire or any other risk against which the landlord may have insured; and

(v) Upon the yielding up of possession of the premises by the tenant at the end of the term return to the tenant the deposit (less any proper deductions) with simple interest calculated at the rate of 5% per annum.

If:

(i) Any part of the rent is in arrears for more than 21 days whether formally demanded or not; or

(ii) If there is any breach of any of the tenant's obligations under this agreement; or

(iii) If the premises are, without the agreement of the landlord, left unoccupied for a continuous period in excess of four weeks, the landlord may re-enter the premises and thereupon the tenancy created by this agreement will determine, but without prejudice to any other rights and remedies of the landlord.

Signed by the landlord...

Landlord's signature witnessed by [name and address]

Signed by witness...

Signed by the tenant...

Tenant's signature witnessed by [name and address]

Signed by witness...

LANDLORD'S NOTICE PROPOSING A NEW RENT UNDER AN ASSURED PERIODIC TENANCY

Housing Act 1988, section 13

• Please write clearly in black ink

• Do not use this form if there is a current rent fixing mechanism in the tenancy.

• Do not use this form to propose a rent adjustment for a statutory periodic tenancy solely because of a proposed change of terms under section 6(2) of the Housing Act 1988.

• This notice may also be used to propose a new rent or licence fee for an assured agricultural occupancy. In such a case references to "landlord"/"tenant" can be read as references to "licensor"/"licensee etc

• This notice proposes a new rent. If you want to oppose this proposal you must keep to the time limit set out in paragraph 2. Read this notice carefully. If you need help or advice take it immediately to:
  • a Citizens' Advice Bureau,
  • a housing aid centre,
  • a law centre,
  • or a solicitor

• Do not use this form to propose an interim increase of rent under an assured periodic tenancy or agricultural occupancy on account of council tax

105

1. To:.. *Name(s)*
of tenant(s)
   Of... *Address*
of premises

2. This is to give notice that from........................19.......
your landlord proposes to charge a new rent
The new rent must take effect at the beginning of a new period of the tenancy and not
earlier than any of the following-

(a)   the minimum period after this notice was served
        (The minimum period is-
        •in the case of a yearly tenancy, six months.
        •in the case of a tenancy where the period is less than a month, one month, and,
        •in any other case, a period equal to the first period of the tenancy)

(b)   the first anniversary of the start of the first period of the tenancy except in the case
        of-
        •a statutory periodic tenancy, which arises when a fixed term assured tenancy ends,
        or
        •an assured tenancy which arose on the death of a tenant under a regulated
        tenancy.

(c)   if the rent under the tenancy has previously been increased by a notice under
        section 13 or a determination under section 14 of the housing Act 1988, the first
        anniversary of the date on which the increased rent took effect.

3. The existing rent is   †.......per....................*e.g. week, month, year*
[This includes council tax*
This includes rates*]

4. The proposed new rent will be   †........per..................*e.g. week, month, year*
This includes council tax*
This includes rates*

If you are required to include in your rent payments for council tax and you refer this
notice to a rent assessment committee, the rent the committee determines will be inclusive
of council tax.

*Cross out if these do not apply

5.   The landlord or superior landlord pays council tax in respect of the property*
        Council tax is not payable in respect of the property*
        A landlord may be liable for council tax if the property is in multiple occupation,
        unless the dwelling is an exempt dwelling.
        The main exemption is where the residents of such a dwelling are students or recent
        school or college leavers

*Cross out if this does not apply

●If you agree with the new rent proposed do nothing. If you do not agree and you are unable to reach agreement with your landlord or do not want to discuss it directly with him, you may refer the notice to your local rent assessment committee before the beginning of the new period given in paragraph 2. The committee will consider your application and will decide whether the proposed new rent is appropriate.

●You will need a special form to refer the notice to a rent assessment committee

To be signed by the landlord or his agent (someone acting for him). If there are joint landlords each landlord or his agent must sign, unless one signs on behalf of the rest with their agreement

Signed...

Names of landlord(s)..

Addresses of landlord(s)...
....
....
Tel...

If signed by agent, name and address of agent.........

Date...............................

Notice to an assured shorthold tenant that the landlord requires possession

To [tenant's name] of [tenant's address]

I [or if notice is given by agent I [name of agent] giving notice on behalf of your landlord(s)] [landlord's name] of [landlord's address] give you notice that I [or the landlord] require possession of [address of premises] by virtue of section 21 of the Housing Act 1988 on or before the day on which a complete period of your tenancy expires after [date at least two months after service of this notice] and that if you do not give up possession of the said dwelling-house to me [or the landlord] on or before that date, I [or the landlord] will commence court proceedings for possession.

Date..

THE LANDLORDS' AND TENANTS' HANDBOOK

Signed...

[*If appropriate* The name and address of the agent who served this notice is.....]

Notice to quit addressed to tenant

To [*tenant's name*] of [*tenant's address*]

I/We [*or if notice is given by agent* I/we (name of agent) giving notice on behalf of your landlord(s)] [*landlord's name*] of [*landlord's address*] give you notice to quit and deliver up possession to him of [*address of let premises*] on [*date*] or the day on which a complete period of your tenancy expires next after the end of four weeks from the service of this notice

Date............

Signed..............

[*if appropriate* The name and address of the agent who served this notice is.....]

Information for tenant

1 If the tenant of licensee does not leave the dwelling, the landlord or licensor must get an order for possession from the court before the tenant or licensee can lawfully be evicted. The landlord or licensor cannot apply for such an order before the notice to quit or notice to determine has run out.

2 A tenant or licensee who does not know if he has any right to remain in possession after a notice to determine runs out can obtain advice from a solicitor. Help with all or part of the cost of legal advice and assistance may be available under the Legal Aid Scheme. He should also be able to obtain information from a Citizens' Advice Bureau, a Housing Aid Centre or a rent officer.

Notes
1 Notice to quit any premises let as a dwelling must be given at least four weeks before it is to take effect and it must be in writing (Protection from Eviction Act 1977, s5).

2 Where a notice to quit is given by a landlord to determine a tenancy of any premises let as a dwelling, the notice must contain this information (The Notices to Quit etc (Prescribed Information) Regulations 1988 (SI No 2201).

Notice seeking possession of a property let on an assured tenancy

Housing Act 1988, section 8

●Please write clearly in black ink

●Do not use this form if possession is sought from an assured shorthold tenant under section 21 of the Housing Act 1988 or if the property is occupied under an assured agricultural occupancy.

●If you need advice about this notice and what you should do about it, take it as quickly as possible to:
●a Citizens' Advice Bureau,
●a housing aid centre,
●a law centre,
●or a solicitor
You may be able to get Legal Aid but this will depend upon your personal circumstances.

● This notice is the first step towards requiring you to give up possession of your home. You should read it very carefully.

1. To:.................................... *name of tenant*

2. Your landlord intends to apply to the court for an order requiring you to give up possession of-

.... *address of premises*
....
....

●If you have an assured tenancy under the Housing Act 1988, which is not an assured shorthold tenancy, you could be required to leave your home if your landlord gets an order for possession from the court on one of the grounds which are set out in Schedule 2 to the Act.

●If you are willing to up possession of your home without a court order, you should tell the person who signed this notice as soon as possible and say when you can leave.

3.The landlord intends to seek possession on ground(s).........in Schedule 2 to the Housing Act 1988, which reads

THE LANDLORDS' AND TENANTS' HANDBOOK

Give the full text of each ground which is being relied on. (Continue on a separate sheet if necessary.)

●Whichever grounds are set out in paragraph 3 the court may allow any of the other grounds to be added at a later date. If this is done, you will be told about it so you can discuss the additional grounds at the court hearing as well as the grounds set out in paragraph 3.

4. Particulars of each ground are as follows-
    give a full explanation of why each ground is being relied upon. (Continue on a separate sheet if necessary).
....
....
....

●If the court is satisfied that any of grounds 1 to 8 is established it must make an order (but see below in respect of fixed term tenancies)

●Before the court will grant an order on any of grounds 9 to 16, it must be satisfied that it is reasonable to require you to leave. this means that, if one of these grounds is set out in paragraph 3, you will be able to suggest to the court that it is not reasonable that you should have to leave, even if you accept that the ground applies.

●The court will not make an order under grounds 1,3 to 7, 9 or 16 to take effect during the fixed term of the tenancy; and it will only make an order during the fixed term on grounds 2, 8 or 10 to 15 if the terms of the tenancy make provision for it to be brought to an end on any of these grounds.

●Where the court makes an order for possession solely on ground 6 or 9, your landlord or licensor must pay your reasonable removal expenses.

5. The court proceedings will not begin until after
....19.....
    Give the date after which court proceedings can be brought

●Where the landlord or licensor is seeking possession under grounds 1,2,5 to 7 or 9 in Schedule 2, court proceedings cannot begin earlier than two months from the date this notice is served on you and not before the date on which the tenancy or licence (had it not been an assured agricultural) could have been brought to an end by a notice to quit or determine served at the same time as this notice.

●Where the landlord or licensor is seeking possession on grounds 3, 4, 8 or 10 to 15, court proceedings cannot begin until two weeks after the date this notice is served.

●After the date shown in paragraph 5, court proceedings may be begun at once but not later than 12 months from the date that this notice is served. After this time the notice will lapse and a new notice must be served before possession can be sought.

To be signed by the landlord or his agent (someone acting for him). If there are joint landlords each landlord or his agent must sign, unless one signs on behalf of the rest with their agreement

Signed..

Names of landlord(s)..

Addresses of landlord(s)..
....
Tel..

If signed by agent, name and address of agent............

Date..

GROUNDS TO BE INSERTED ON NOTICE SEEKING POSSESSION

Ground 1

Not later than the beginning of the tenancy the landlord gave notice in writing to the tenant that possession might be recovered on this ground or the court is of the opinion that it is just and equitable to dispense with the requirement of notice and (in either case)
(a) at some time before the beginning of the tenancy, the landlord who is seeking possession or in the case of joint landlords seeking possession, at least one of them occupied the dwelling-house as his only or principal home, or
(b) the landlord who is seeking possession or in the case of joint landlords seeking possession at least one of them requires the dwelling-house as his or his spouse's only or principal home and neither the landlord (or, in the case of joint landlords any one of them) nor any other person who, as landlord, derived title under the landlord who gave the notice mentioned above acquired the reversion on the tenancy for money or money's worth.

Ground 2

The dwelling-house is subject to a mortgage granted before the beginning of the tenancy and-
(a) the mortgagee is entitled to exercise a power of sale conferred upon him by the mortgage or by s101 of the Law of Property Act 1925; and
(b) the mortgagee requires possession of the dwelling-house for the purpose of disposing of it with vacant possession in exercise of that power; and
(c) either notice was given as aforementioned in ground 1 above or the court is satisfied that it is just and equitable to dispense with the requirement of notice;

and for the purpose of this ground "mortgage" includes a charge and mortgagee shall be construed accordingly.

Ground 8
Both at the date of the service of the notice under section 8 of this Act relating to the proceedings for possession and at the date of the hearing-
(a) if rent is payable weekly or fortnightly at least thirteen weeks' rent is unpaid;
(b) if the rent is payable monthly, at least three months' rent is unpaid;
(c) if the rent is payable quarterly, at least one quarter's rent is more than three months in arrears; and
(d) if the rent is payable yearly, at least three months' rent is more than three months in arrears
and for the purpose of this ground "rent" means rent lawfully due from the tenant.

Ground 9
Suitable alternative accommodation is available for the tenant or will be available for him when the possession order takes effect

Ground 10
Some rent lawfully due from the tenant-
(a) is unpaid on the date on which proceedings for possession are begun; and
(b) except where subsection (1) (b) of section 8 applies, was in arrears at the date of the service of the notice under that section relating to the proceedings.

Ground 11
Whether or not any rent is in arrears on the date on which proceedings for possession are begun, the tenant has persistently delayed in paying rent which has become lawfully due

Ground 12
Any obligation of the tenancy (other than one related to the payment of rent) has been broken or not performed.

Ground 13
The condition of the dwelling house or any of the common parts has deteriorated owing to acts of waste by, or the neglect or default of, the tenant or any other person residing in the dwelling-house and, in the case of an act of waste by, or the neglect or default of, a person lodging with the tenant or a sub-tenant of his, the tenant has not taken such steps as he ought reasonably to have taken for the removal of the lodge or the sub-tenant.

For the purpose of this ground, "common parts" means any part of a building comprising the dwelling-house and any other premises which the tenant is entitled under the terms of the tenancy to use in common with the occupiers of other dwelling-houses in which the landlord has an interest or estate.

Ground 14
The tenant or any person residing with in the dwelling-house has been guilty of conduct which is a nuisance or annoyance to the adjoining occupiers, or has been convicted of using the dwelling-house or allowing the dwelling-house to be used for immoral or illegal purposes.

Ground 15
The condition of any furniture provided for use under the tenancy has, in the opinion of the court, deteriorated, owing to ill-treatment by the tenant or any other person residing in the dwelling-house and, in the case of ill-treatment by a person lodging with the tenant or a sub-tenant of his, the tenant has not taken such steps as he ought reasonably to have taken for the removal of the lodger or sub-tenant.

Ground 16
The dwelling was let to the tenant in consequence of his employment by the landlord seeking possession or a previous landlord under the tenancy and the tenant has ceased to be in that employment.

For the purposes of this ground, at a time when the landlord is or was the Secretary of State, employment by a health service body, as defined in s60(7) of the National Health Service and Community Care Act 1990, shall be regarded as employment by the Secretary of State.

12. LEGAL SOURCES AND FURTHER READING

Acts of Parliament

Most of the law discussed in this book comes from two Acts of Parliament:

- The Rent Act 1977; and
- The Housing Act 1988.

The Rent Act governs tenancies granted before 15 January 1989, the Housing Act those granted on that day or afterwards. There is a small overlap between the provisions of the two Acts, usually in relation to a tenant who was granted a new tenancy by the same landlord of the same property after that date although he had been a tenant before, and when a tenant dies.

Other relevant Acts of Parliament include:

- The Protection from Eviction Act 1977, which specifies the rules dealing with wrongful eviction and harassment;
- The County Courts Act 1984, which specifies the procedure for bringing actions in the county court;
- The Landlord and Tenant Act 1985, which in sections 11 to 15 specifies the rules about repairs of residential property;
- The Landlord and Tenant Act 1987, which in section 47 specifies the requirement for a notice giving the landlord's name and address; and
- The Accommodation Agencies Act 1953, which prohibits the charging by agencies of fees to tenants until after they have been found a property.

12. LEGAL SOURCES AND FURTHER READING

Statutory instruments

In addition there are *statutory instruments* or *secondary legislation*. These deal with matters of detail. They are nominally passed by Parliament but usually without any debate or discussion. Acts of Parliament give the authority to minsters to make such instruments. Where a certain form has to be used to, for instance, end a tenancy, the wording of that form will have been specified in a statutory instrument. Similarly most of the county court's procedure is set out in such instruments rather than the County Courts Act itself.

Case law

Where an Act of Parliament does not deal with a specific point or is ambiguous on it, it is for the courts to decide what the law is. Once a court has made a decision that is said to create a *precedent*, which is normally binding on other courts considering the same point. The most important (relatively) recent case in the field of residential tenancies was *Street v Mountford* in 1985 (see pages 22). Other examples of important decisions have been:

- *Hampstead Way Investments v Lewis-Weare* 1985 (what constitutes a person's home);
- *Love and Lugg v Herrity* 1990 (effect of assured tenant giving up possession); and
- *Tagro v Cafane* 1991 (damages for wrongful eviction).

Cases which do set precedents in this way are reported in the *Law Reports*.

Textbooks

Lawyers researching a point of law will usually start with a text book. The leading books on Landlord and Tenant Law are both known by the names of their original authors: *Woodfall* and *Hill and Redman*, respectively. They are edited and regularly updated by practising barristers. Each of these works runs to several looseleaf volumes. *Woodfall* costs £260 and *Hill and Redman* £415. They are available for reference in many public libraries. Neither is particularly easy to find one's way around, *Hill & Redman* is set out in a marginally more logical way.

All the relevant Acts of Parliament and statutory instruments are set out in Butterworth's *Landlord and Tenant Handbook*, which is a bargain by the standards of law books at £32-50.

Other books which might be of assistance to lay-people attempting to grapple with landlord and tenant problems include:

●*Residential Possession Proceedings* by Gary Webber, published by Longman for £45 (a detailed guide to possession proceedings, including actions by mortgagees as well as tenants);

●*Residential Tenancies* by Richard Colbey, published by Longman for £13-95 (a short guide to the law relating to the area generally but written in 1990 and now out of date in some particulars);

●*Defending Possession Proceedings* by Jan Luba, Nic Madge and Derek McConnell, published by Legal Action for £32 (covers a similar area to Webber's book and despite its title of assistance to landlords as well as tenants); and

●*Drafting Residential Leases* by Charles Bennett, published by Longman for £42 (a guide to the legal side of granting a tenancy but written in 1990 and now out of date in some particulars).

The *County Court Practice*, often known as the *Green Book*, is published annually in May. This contains the definitive account of all the county court procedural rules as well as an account of many areas of substantive law, including residential tenancies. The 1994 edition cost £135. It is available in most libraries and it can be possible to pick up slightly out of date editions relatively cheaply: local solicitors might oblige. In the context of possession actions though pre-1994 editions, which do not incorporate the recent procedural changes (see pages 89 to 90), are of limited value.

The best legal textbook for people seeking to understand the mysteries of legal procedure is *Civil Litigation* by John O'Hare and Robert Hill published by Longman for £26.

Fitzwarren Publishing intends bringing out a layperson's guide to conducting litigation in the middle of 1995.

GLOSSARY

assignment: the transfer of a tenancy from one person to another.

assured tenancy: a residential tenancy granted after 14 January 1989.

bailiff: a court official whose task it is to enforce court orders including those for eviction (*q.v.*).

break clause: a provision in a tenancy that enables either the landlord or the tenant to terminate it before the term (*q.v.*) expires.

Case 11 tenancy: a tenancy granted before 15 January 1989 where the landlord served a notice saying the property had previously been his home and that he intended living there again in the future.

counterclaim: a claim made by the defendant (*q.v.*) in court proceedings.

covenant: a term often used to describe the promises given in the lease by the landlord and the tenant.

defence: the formal document filed by the defendant (*q.v.*) in court proceedings, may also contain a counterclaim (*q.v.*).

defendant: the person against whom court proceedings are brought, occasionally the term respondent is used instead.

demised premises: the property that is the subject matter of a tenancy.

deposit: a payment by a tenant to a landlord to secure the tenant's performance of his obligations including paying rent and not causing any damage.

"DSS tenants": sometimes used to describe tenants whose rent is paid entirely by housing benefit (*q.v.*). The name derives from the Department of Social Security which is largely responsible for funding housing benefit, although this is actually administered by local authorities.

eviction: the act of removing a person from a property. If it is done without a court order it is almost certainly a wrongful eviction (*q.v.*).

exclusive possession: the right to occupy property to the exclusion of everyone else; this is the defining feature of a tenancy.

fair rent: a rent assessed by a rent officer (*q.v.*) in respect of a tenancy subject to the Rent Act 1977.

fixtures and fittings: things that although not an integral part of a property that are attached to it, unlike furniture which is removable.

Fitted carpets obviously are fittings as is the wall-paper. Rugs though are not, nor are unfitted wardrobes however heavy and difficult to move.

forfeiture: when a landlord decrees that a tenancy has come to an end because the tenant has broken the terms of it or not paid the rent, and a forfeiture clause (*q.v.*) permits him to do so.

forfeiture clause: a clause in a tenancy agreement saying that the landlord is entitled to treat the tenant as having forfeited the lease if he breaks its terms or does not pay the rent.

freehold: absolute ownership of property. Most house owners are freeholders, but most flats are let on long leases (*q.v.*).

Ground 1 tenancy: a tenancy granted after 14 January 1989, where the landlord served a notice saying the property had previously been his home or that he intended living there again in the future.

ground rent: a rent paid by a lessee under a long lease, usually of a nominal annual amount to the freeholder.

Housing Act 1988: the Act of Parliament under which the Rent Acts (*q.v.*) were repealed in respect of tenancies subsequent to 14 January 1989 and by which another regime, generally less favourable to tenants, was substituted.

housing benefit: a form of social security administered by local authorities to help relatively poor people pay their rent.

injunction: an order made by a court compelling someone to do something e.g. carry out repairs, or refrain from doing something e.g. harassing a tenant.

joint and several liability: a form of agreement under which two or more tenants are each liable in respect of the breaches of other tenants' as well as their own.

"key money": sometimes used as another word for premium (*q.v.*) for a short term tenancy.

lease: an agreement under which someone agrees to let another have exclusive possession (*q.v.*) of a property.

legal aid: government funding for lawyers to represent poorer people in legal proceedings.

licence: an agreement under which one person allows another to occupy property, but which does not amount to a tenancy (*q.v.*), usually because exclusive possession (*q.v.*) is not given.

licensee: someone who is given a licence (*q.v.*) to occupy property.

licensor: someone who licenses another person to occupy property.

licence fee: the correct term for "rent" (*q.v.*) paid under a licence (*q.v.*).

lodger: a person paying to live in another person's home, almost always a licensee (*q. v.*).

long lease: usually used to refer to a lease of longer than 21 years. Usually the rent under such a lease will be a nominal ground rent (*q. v.*) but a substantial premium will be required for the grant or assignment of such a lease.

mesne profits: the sum payable by a tenant who has continued living at a property after his tenancy has ended, usually equivalent to the rent he was paying before the tenancy ended.

monthly tenancy: a periodic tenancy (*q. v.*) where rent is payable monthly.

mortgage: the right over property given by an owner who is lent money, usually by a building society or a bank, on the security of that property.

mortgagee: the person granting the mortgage (*q. v.*) in exchange for being lent money, i.e. the property owner.

mortgagor: a person (or, more usually, institution) lending money secured on property.

notice to quit: a notice served by a landlord or a tenant on the other party announcing their intention of ending a tenancy.

particulars of claim: a plaintiff's (*q. v.*) written statement of what he is alleging and claiming, set out when he commences court proceedings.

"paying guest": another term for lodger (*q. v.*).

periodic tenancy: a tenancy which is not for a fixed term, but which is automatically renewed every time the tenant pays his rent for the period that rent covers, such as a week, month or quarter.

plaintiff: the person who commences court proceedings by making a claim, in some circumstances referred to as the applicant.

possession order: the order made by the court requiring a person to leave property.

premium: a payment made by a tenant in consideration of the grant or assignment of a tenancy. For residential tenancies where a market rent is paid these are normally not required. The substantial payment made when someone buys a long lease on a flat is a premium.

protected shorthold tenancy: a tenancy granted after 14 January 1989 for a term in excess of six months, during which time the landlord cannot terminate the tenancy, and in respect of which the landlord has served the appropriate notice.

protected tenancy: a residential tenancy granted before 15 January 1989. Once the tenancy has expired or the landlord has served notice to quit (*q.v.*) it becomes a statutory tenancy (*q.v.*).

Protection from Eviction Act 1977: the Act of Parliament which provides serious civil and criminal sanctions against a landlord who harasses or wrongfully evicts a tenant.

quiet enjoyment: the tenant's right to enjoy the demised premises (*q.v.*) without the landlord interfering with him.

rent: the payment by a tenant in consideration for being able to occupy property for a certain period under a tenancy.

Rent Acts: the series of Acts of Parliament culminating in the Rent Act 1977 under which tenants were given extensive security of tenure and rent control. Repealed in respect of most subsequent tenancies by the Housing Act 1988 (*q.v.*).

rent assessment committee: a committee, usually chaired by a lawyer, which conducts most official rent assessment other than that which is the rent officer's (*q.v.*) responsibility.

rent book: a book provided by the landlord but kept by the tenant which the landlord signs as a receipt for each payment of rent made by the tenant.

rent officer: an official whose primary job is the setting of fair rents (*q.v.*) in respect of tenancies granted before 15 January 1989.

restricted contract: a tenancy granted before 15 January 1989 under which the landlord and the tenant live in the same building.

secure tenancy: a residential tenancy granted by a local authority.

security of tenure: the right a tenant may acquire to stay in possession of premises after the contractual term of his tenancy has expired

service licence: a licence (*q.v.*) granted to somebody to live in property, which is essential to enable that person to perform his employment duties.

service occupancy: another term for a service licence (*q.v.*).

"sitting tenant": a person who has acquired statutory protection particularly under the Rent Acts (*q.v.*) and cannot be removed by his landlord.

"squatter": a person who has moved into property without ever having the permission of anyone entitled to give him such permission.

statutory assured tenancy: the tenancy that arises after an assured tenancy has ended.

statutory tenancy: the tenancy that arises after a protected tenancy (*q.v.*) has ended.

subletting: the letting by a tenant of some or all of the demised premises (*q.v.*) to another tenant.

surety: a person who agrees to pay a debt if the person, such as the tenant, principally liable should default on it.

tenancy: an agreement under which one person, a landlord, grants to another, a tenant, the right to exclusive possession (*q.v.*) of property for a specified term or renewable period.

term: the length of time for which a tenancy is granted.

warrant of possession: the order given by the court to the bailiffs instructing them to evict, physically if necessary, people from property after a possession order (*q.v.*) has been made.

weekly tenancy: a periodic tenancy (*q.v.*) where rent is payable weekly.

wrongful eviction: the act of unlawfully evicting a person from a property. Evictions (*q.v.*) are normally only lawful if carried out by a bailiff pursuant to a court order.

INDEX

RESIDENTIAL LETTINGS

LOCK
═ESTATES═

Based on Camden High Street, in the social centre of North London, Lock Estates have been involved in residential lettings for over 20 years. We have a wealth of experience in dealing with all aspects of property management: matching up the ideal property, tenant and landlord - inventories - value for money maintenance - rent collection - quarterly inspections: these are only a few of the services we provide.

We cover properties in North and South London, and specialise in the Camden and the surrounding areas: from Euston to Archway - St John's Wood to Islington.

For tenants and landlords alike, we offer the peace of mind that comes with our longstanding and proven track record, coupled with our wide experience in all property matters.

Our sales department can also offer advice to prospective first time buyers, as well as free valuations of their properties to landlords: for whom we have sold many of their properties to homebuyers, investors and property companies.

Please feel free to either telephone us, or come in to our office, where our experienced staff will be able to discuss your particular requirements with you.

Residential Lettings - Sales - Property Management
Commercial - Investment - Development

0171-482 2222

EST 1852

LANDLORDS

The Property Management Department of Drivers and Norris has been in the field of caring for people's properties for over 100 years, whether it is your intention of going abroad for a few years, letting a home you have inherited or letting in preference to selling, it is a comfort to leave it in experienced hands.

Management.

Please call us now for a free inspection

071 607 4040

TEL: 071-607 4040
407-409 Holloway Rd, N7 6HP

Association of Residential
Letting Agents

Luxury apartment in North West London...

...cottage in the Cotswolds...

MAKE US YOUR FIRST CHOICE

We have many tenants seeking quality property
in London and the Home Counties, and the experience to
match your property with the right people.
If you're looking to let, we'll be delighted to help you.
For a professional service ring one of our offices now!

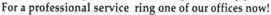

The Chancellors
Group of Estate Agents Ltd

Anscombe & Ringland Offices at **BATTERSEA** 0171 924 5022 • **FINCHLEY** 0181 349 3320 **HAMPSTEAD** 0171 794 1151
HIGHGATE 0181 340 2600 • **KENSINGTON** 0171 727 7227 • **ST. JOHN'S WOOD** 0171 722 7101 • **STANMORE** 0181 954 6111

Kathini Graham **KNIGHTSBRIDGE** 0171 584 3285

Chancellors Offices at **ABINGDON** 01235 532420 • **ASCOT** 01344 872909 • **HEADINGTON** 01865 65000
HENLEY on THAMES 01491 571157 • **HIGH WYCOMBE** 01494 462057 • **KINGSTON upon THAMES** 0181 546 3131
MAIDENHEAD 01628 31031 • **NEWBURY** 01635 31915 • **NORTHWOOD** 01923 833544 • **OXFORD** 01865 724881
RICHMOND 0181 940 2255 • **SUMMERTOWN** 01865 516161 • **SUNNINGDALE** 01344 876487
WEYBRIDGE 01932 856334 • **WITNEY** 01993 774179 **WOKING** 01483 756648

Russell Baldwin & Bright **HEREFORD** 01432 266663

ESTATE AGENTS • RESIDENTIAL LETTINGS & PROPERTY MANAGEMENT
SURVEYORS & VALUERS

Park Lettings Ltd

~ Residential Lettings ~

We urgently require properties
in all London areas.
We have a variety of excellent
tenants awaiting to rent your property.

• FREE MANAGEMENT •

For a limited period we are offering
FREE MANAGEMENT

Please call on the number below
and ask for ext : 2021 or 2059

PARK LETTINGS LTD
Premier House
2 Gayton Road
Harrow. Middlesex HA1 2XU
Tel : 081 863 9001